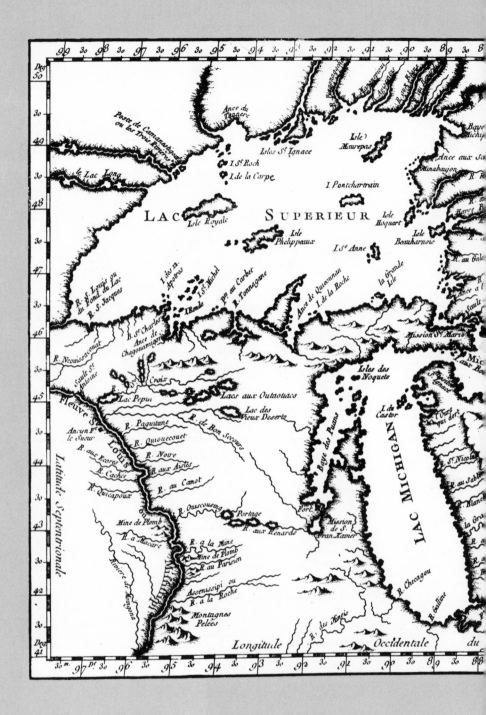

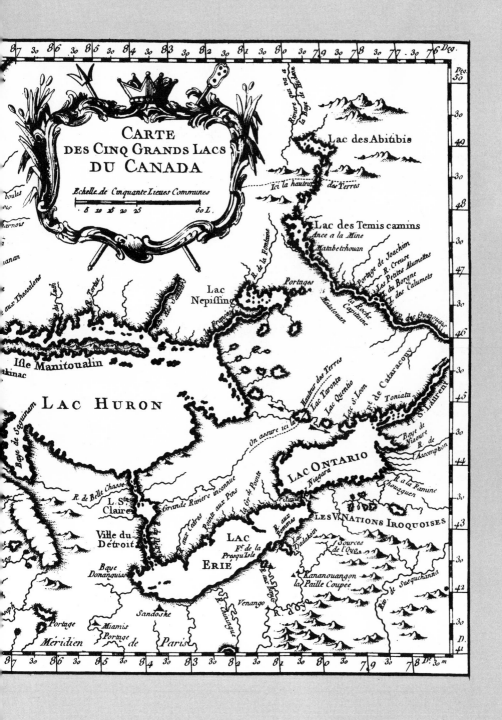

CARTE
DES CINQ GRANDS LACS
DU CANADA

Echelle de Cinquante Lieues Communes

5 10 15 20 25   60 L.

Riviere qui va a la Baye de Hudson

Lac des Abitibis

Ici la hauteur des Terres

Lac des Temiscamins

Ance a la Mine

Matabetchouan

Portage de Joachim

R. Creuse

Les Petites Alumettes
du Borgne
des Calumets

Lac
Nepissing

Portages

Maskouan

La Roche Capitaine

R. des Outaouais

boules

arnois

anan

aux Thealones

du Lech

du Torket

des Francois

Francois

R. de la Fontaine

Isle Manitoualin

hinac

LAC HURON

Hauteur des Terres

Lac Taronto

Lac Quenbo

Isle S. Leon

Fort de Cataracoui

Toniata

On assure ici la

Baye de Niaouré

R. de l'Assomption

Baye de Saguinam

R. de Belle Chasse

L. S.te Claire

Grande Riviere inconnue

aux Cedres

Pointe aux Pins

Mer de Pointe

LAC ONTARIO

Niagara

Baldwin

R. aux Pommes

Lac Tjadakoin

A la Famine
Choueguen

LES V. NATIONS IROQUOISES

Ville du Détroit

LAC
Ft. de la Presqu'Isle

ERIE

Baye Donanquissé

R. aux Boeufs

Sources de l'Oue

Kananouangon
la Paille Coupee

Fin de Susquehanna

Venango

R. d'O

R. Chiarague

Sandoske

Meridien

Portage

Miamis

Portage de Paris

S.t Laurent

PONTIAC,

King of the Great Lakes

Other Books by Clide Hollmann

THE EAGLE FEATHER
FIVE ARTISTS OF THE OLD WEST
Hastings House

PARTNERS ON THE SANTE FE TRAIL
Westminster Press

PONTIAC,
King of the
Great Lakes

by
CLIDE HOLLMANN

HASTINGS HOUSE PUBLISHERS, INC.

New York

FOR JEAN
who encouraged me in writing this book

Published simultaneously in Canada
by Saunders, of Toronto, Ltd., Don Mills, Ontario.

Library of Congress Catalog Card Number: 68-13443
Printed in the United States of America

CONTENTS

LIST OF ILLUSTRATIONS

Major Henry Gladwyn
    Painting by John Holland
    From the Library of Congress, Photoduplication Service
Indians Playing Lacrosse
    Painting by George Catlin
    From New York Public Library, Prints Division
A Plan of Fort Detroit, 1760
    From Burton Historical Division, Detroit Public Library,
    Courtesy of James M. Babcock, Chief
    Reproduced by Copy Craft, Inc., Detroit, Michigan
The Death of Pontiac
    Painting by De Cost Smith
    From *The Conspiracy of Pontiac* by Francis Parkman
    Courtesy of Little, Brown and Company, Publishers, Boston

PREFACE

There are many versions of the Pontiac story, each one differing in details such as spelling of names and places, dates and incidents.

One of the reasons for the differences is that the surviving documents of that period (journals, diaries, letters, military reports and other papers) are handwritten in French or English, and the spidery penmanship of the time is difficult, sometimes impossible, to read or translate.

After two centuries the discrepancies in the versions multiply and the line of demarkation separating fact from fiction becomes dim.

However, it is well established that Pontiac, the great chief of the Ottawas and leader of the Great Lakes tribes, planned and carried out the first organized effective resistance to the white man ever attempted by Indians.

His war proved to be one of the most significant events in the early history of our country.

Chief Pontiac became a legend in his own time and his stature as patriot and stout-hearted fighter for the rights of his people has not grown less through the years.

1

PONTIAC

SOMETIME BETWEEN 1718 and 1720 in the area of Michilimackinac (The Great Turtle) on the north shore of Lake
Michigan, a husky Indian baby was born and announced his
arrival with a loud squawk.

His aged grandmother shook her sides in silent laughter
but neither she nor any of the others in the lodge foresaw
that the little squawker would some day become the great
Pontiac, chief of the Ottawas, leader of the Great Lakes
tribes, and the most important Indian of his time.

The name was originally Obwandiyag, pronounced
Brondiak. There were many different versions of the name
such as *Pondiyak* and *Pontdiac*, but it finally emerged as
Pontiac.

His father was an Ottawa chief and a member of the
Otter clan. His mother belonged to the Ojibway tribe. Spoken in rapid French, the name Ojibway became Chippewa:
thus the same tribe was known by two names. Being related
to both the Chippewa and the Ottawa tribes later enabled

11

Pontiac to draw on both for support. In the Algonquin language, which the Ottawas used, Ottawa means *to trade*.

Little has been recorded of Pontiac's boyhood but it is known that he grew up in the Ottawa village of his father and learned to hunt and swim, paddle a canoe and play lacrosse with the other youngsters. He was a champion as a youth and kept up his athletic pursuits during his long and active life, often paddling his own canoe while his accompanying warriors relaxed.

Lessons in making war were an integral part of the training every young Indian received. Pontiac was an apt pupil. He learned to track an enemy through an almost impenetrable forest without stirring a leaf, to plan his capture and to raise the scalp, unaided.

While other young Indians were shooting their arrows at trees for practice, the young Ottawa was developing the war skills that later brought him the leadership of his own tribe and many others.

Only a few facts are known about Pontiac's family. In 1768 he implied in a letter that he had a wife from one of the Illinois tribes. The identity of his first wife is not known but he had other wives at various times. (Most of the chiefs and many of the warriors had plural wives. There seemed to be no jealousy on this account — the women shared the work load and possibly the rough treatment alloted to them in the man's world of the Indian.) Kentuckeegun, allegedly one of Pontiac's widows, lived in the Ottawa village at the mouth of the Maumee in 1807.

As for his children, little is known, but Pontiac's son, Shegenaba, was reported to have made a speech in 1775. Another son, Otussa, was buried on the Maumee. Atoka, a descendant, was chief of the Ottawa village on the Maumee and later moved west of the Mississippi.

A recent news item dated February 2, 1967, reports that

Scott W. Williams, who played Chief Thunder Cloud in the movies and Tonto on the radio, was a direct descendant of Chief Pontiac of the Ottawas. He died in the Veterans Hospital in Chicago at age 68. He was the first American Indian to enlist in the United States Army in World War I.

In appearance Pontiac was big and imposing, stately in manner and convincing in speech. His body was tattooed as was the custom. He also painted his face for ceremonials. He wore his hair in short pompadour, diminishing in height from front to back. The chief often wore beads in his ears, a stone in his nose, a bearclaw necklace, and many bands of shells or precious fur on his arms, with a few feathers in his hair.

In summer his costume was a shirt and a breechcloth — or just a breechcloth. In winter he usually wore moccasins, deerskin leggings reaching to his thighs, a breechcloth, a highly colored shirt bought from a trader, a coat of English or French make, and a short blanket called a "stroud." In extremely cold weather a fur wrap was added.

However, when on the warpath or waiting to ambush a foe, all ornamentation was laid aside and the chief was just another warrior wearing only moccasins, breechcloth and a single eagle feather in his short hair.

Pontiac claimed the entire Great Lakes region as his home. As a child he played on the shores. As a youth he paddled his birch-bark canoe from lake to lake and hunted in the forests. In manhood he saw the lakes as a beautiful five-pointed star set down in his homeland. His feeling for them was one of gratitude for the food contained in the waters and forests, and a sense of awe toward the beauty and mystery of sparkling blue-green waters against the dark green of the mighty trees that rimmed them. He often told his warriors that the Master-of-Life had created the Great Lakes country for his red children and they must keep it for their own forever.

Within their tribal lands the Indians moved with the wild

game. They were meat-eaters and when the game became scarce in one area, they moved to another spot to allow nature to restock the land with animals; but they always stayed close to their beloved lakes where there was fish to eat and to store for the long winters, and wild rice growing along the creeks to be harvested by the squaws.

It was all Indian country when Jacques Cartier sailed up the St. Lawrence River in 1535 and it was still Indian country in 1760 with only a few white men in the forts and fur-trading posts scattered along the shores of the lakes and rivers.

Indians and French Canadians

During the French and Indian War, while the English and the French were fighting on Indian territory for Indian furs and Indian lands, it was inevitable that the tribes should become involved. Both nations recruited Indian forces, bands and individuals, for scout duty, to carry out raids and to ambush troops.

Because of their early association with the French explorers and fur traders, beginning with the founding of Quebec in 1608, most of the Algonquins, including Pontiac's tribe, the Ottawas, were allies of the French and fought with them throughout the war in which Canada and the French forts were lost to the British.*

Pontiac was called a savage, naturally cunning and treacherous but possessing great ability. He was gifted with a brilliant style of speaking that won him the allegiance of his hearers and the respect of his own warriors.

An unknown artist painted a purported likeness of Pontiac many years later and captioned his work, *Pontiac, The Red Napoleon.*

In the masterly conquest of their different worlds, and in the tragic circumstances of their deaths, the two leaders, the painted war-chief and the dandified French emperor, Napoleon Bonaparte, were not unlike.

---

* For more information on the situation in this area and the English commanders involved at this time, see the Addenda at the end of the book.

2

PONTIAC'S INDIAN HERITAGE

IN THE GREAT LAKES AREA, as in other Indian communities, the tribes had no printed laws, charters or constitutions. They were governed by the chiefs in accordance with long-established customs and by decisions reached in councils.

The civil chief or sachem was the leader who directed the councils of the tribe and governed in time of peace. The office, which allowed him only to advise and counsel and then consent to the majority rule, was hereditary.

The war-chief was the military leader. He planned the strategy and led the warriors to the attack. This authority was acquired by personal merit and prowess in battle. It was not hereditary. Any warrior might become a war-chief, but he had to earn the honor. Sometimes the same man served in both capacities.

Special groups, called clans, also existed in every community. These clans were represented by emblems of beasts, birds or reptiles, called totems. The Bear totem, the Wolf totem and the Hawk totem, along with the Turtle totem, were most prominent and considered most distinguished. Each clan member supposedly took on the virtues of his totem animal, bird or reptile, and wore its insignia in his headdress or about his neck. In doing this he was bound to aid and assist another member of his clan, welcome him into his lodge, share food with him and avenge a wrong done to him.

In the councils and conferences with the white men, the Indians usually addressed the white leaders as Father or Brother. This was a courtesy title of respect or flattery. It did not indicate relationship.

The Indian orator in his speeches was a diplomat of no mean talent. He had a plentiful stock of metaphors; some wildly beautiful, others picturesque, even romantic. He used them to good effect in expressing his ideas:

To make war was to "raise the war whoop" or to "lift the hatchet."

To make peace was to "take the enemy by the hand" or to "take hold of the chain of friendship." Pontiac used the "chain of friendship" expression often.

To deliberate on a matter or reconsider one was to "kindle the council fire."

To pay compensation for a slaying and to receive forgiveness was "covering the bones of the dead."

To ask the white men to "dry the Indians' tears" was a plea for gifts or a distribution of rum.

"Bright sunshine" meant a period of peace, while a "black cloud" symbolized a state of war or a disaster.

To declare an "open path" between nations meant that a state of peace existed.

All these terms were in common use. However, the inspired speaker might make up his own list as his fancy dictated or as the occasion called. for.

Along with his flowery or dramatic words, the Indian orator used wampum. This consisted of small fragments of

The Wampum Maker

clam or snail shells rounded like beads, arranged in patterns and made into belts, bands or strings. The orator, in making a point, delivered a wampum belt to the leader of the party he was addressing to emphasize his words and insure that they would be remembered. After the council the belts were rolled up and stored in the keeping of the elders of the tribe who would reread them and interpret their meaning to the uninstructed.

Wampum was precious to the Indians and was often used as money or as a medium of exchange. It played an important part in their treaties, councils and ceremonies, as agreements made while receiving or giving a wampum belt were always carried out.

The squaws made the belts, which were often works of art and treasured by Indians and whites alike. They were in colors: red, black, green, purple and white — the color determined by the message it carried.

A white belt was a message of peace. A belt of red was a summons asking the tribe to join the senders on the warpath against a common enemy. At friendly meetings it was customary for an Indian tribe, when the other party had lost a chief or a warrior, to give a formal speech of condolence and offer a black belt of wampum in token of mourning.

There are a few belts still in existence, mostly in museums and private collections. The best known is the one the Pennsylvania Indians gave William Penn in 1682 after the "big talk" in which the colonists and the Indians "agreed to warn one another in case either group was in danger. It was further agreed that the friendly feeling of cooperation should be passed on to their children for generations so that peace and friendship might last while the suns and stars endure. This treaty was never broken during the life of William Penn."*

The belt, now kept in Philadelphia, showed the figures of a white man and a red man clasping hands.

Sometimes other gifts such as tobacco, a pipe or a blanket, were given as a substitute for wampum.

The calumet (French for pipe or reed) played an important part in Indian tribal ceremonies, in councils with the whites, and in other meetings. It was a decorated peace pipe made of soft red stone with a long stem adorned with feathers that was passed from hand to hand as the warriors and chiefs sat in a circle before the glowing campfire enjoying puffs of tobacco smoke.

The ritual of the calumet sealed treaties and alliances and bonds of friendship. Often the smoking was followed by a

---

* From *The History of Pennsylvania* by Elmer W. Cressman, D.Ed. New York, N.Y., Noble & Noble Pub., Inc., 1944

The Ritual of the Calumet

calumet dance with the natives leaping, prancing and stamping to the beat of Indian drums.

War was a way of life to the Indian. He wanted invariably to win and all means of obtaining victory were equally honorable. To outwit the enemy or defeat him by trickery was as great an accomplishment or *coup* as to outfight him or conquer him by sheer strength and agility. However, to risk life needlessly was considered the act of a fool. The war-chief who lost a warrior unnecessarily was not honored.

Much has been written about the North American natives eating human flesh and there have been authentic cases cited.

For the most part it appears that even when a hated captive was massacred or burned at the stake, only the heart was cut from the victim's body and eaten as a symbol of triumph.

The favorite menu at most Indian feasts was dog, which the natives preferred above the white man's beef or pork.

Moving from camp or village to a fishing place or to the hunting grounds was no problem to the Great Lakes Indians. They had birchbark canoes, which were both light and strong. The Chippewas, in particular, were noted for their skill in building fine ones.

These craft were frail looking, but the natives rode the rough waters of the lakes in them as the western Indians rode their ponies over the trails and mountain passes.

When they encountered rapids or falls, the Indians took their canoes on their backs and carried them past the danger point before resuming their journey. The French called this "portage," from the French "porter" meaning "to carry."

The natives pushed up rivers in their canoes, and built their villages on the shores and islands where there was always pure water to drink and for household purposes. A warrior had only to drop his canoe into the water and he was on his way to a council, a feast, or some scalp-taking expedition of his own.

Pontiac once led a delegation of chiefs and warriors to an important conference in sixty gaily decorated canoes to show the white men the scope of his power and influence.

3

THE SURRENDER OF DETROIT

IT WAS A COLD, rainy day in November, 1760, when the 200 men of *Rogers' Rangers* beached their twelve whale boats on the shore of Lake Erie and set out to find a camping place.

They were anxious to build a fire and get warm and dry. They were not concerned about who owned the land and forests or the game. They had their own herd of fat cattle following them along the shore.

Suddenly a loud outcry came from the timber ahead. Half-naked Indians, brandishing tomahawks, sprang from behind trees and formed a half circle about the Rangers.

As the Indians continued yelling and making gestures that could only mean STOP, the Rangers halted their search and moved back a few paces. They looked at their commander, Major Robert Rogers, for orders.

The interpreter for the white men signalled for silence, but the natives kept up their clamour. They yelled, "Pondiyak! Pondiyak!" and kept up the din until Rogers stepped out from his men and faced them.

There was an instant hush as the tall, imposing leader of

23

the Rangers stood confidently beside his men and ordered them to make camp where they were.

Rogers, a native of New Hampshire, was on a mission for General Amherst, Commander-in-Chief of the British forces in America. He had been sent to accept the surrender of the forts still flying the French flag and to take possession of them in the name of the British Crown. Although the formal peace treaty had not yet been signed, Amherst wanted to lose no time in claiming the fruits of victory.

The Rangers, an independent company paid from British funds, were composed of hunters, woodsmen and a few farmers whom Rogers had recruited and trained for rugged duty. Armed with Indian weapons such as hatchets and knives as well as English guns, they scouted for the British forces, harassed the French and performed other hazardous duties.

Their leader, Major Robert Rogers, a champion athlete in pioneer sports, was a bold and venturesome veteran of the French and Indian War, brave and firm of purpose but often unresponsive to discipline. His lapses were overlooked because of his successes in planning and carrying out raids and attacks. In fact, both Rogers and his Rangers were as rugged as the times.

Now his commanding presence so impressed the Indians that they waited quietly while the interpreter questioned them.

The tallest of the warriors, still holding his tomahawk aloft, fixed beady, black eyes on the white leader and signalled that this was their land, and their chief, Pondiyak, would not allow the white men to proceed farther until after they had talked with him.

When the interpreter asked about Pondiyak's whereabouts, he was told that the chief was near and would come to meet them.

While the Indians waited, they seated themselves on the ground, seemingly comfortable on the cold, damp earth.

The Rangers lighted a fire and stood about it in small groups, keeping a wary eye on the natives.

Suddenly there was a burst of loud yells from the Indians and Pondiyak strode into the circle of his warriors, giving the Rangers their first look at the powerful leader of all the tribes in the area. The Englishmen immediately dubbed him *Pontiac*.

At that time Chief Pontiac was in his middle forties and at the height of his physical and mental powers. He was dark, even for an Indian, with a strong, intelligent face and the majestic bearing befitting one in command. In addition, as the white men were to learn, Pontiac had a gift of oratory unmatched in his own world and a voice that stirred not only his own people but the white men as well. In looks, words and actions he was indeed, *the king of the Great Lakes*.

Face to face with the durable Rogers, Pontiac boldly asked what the white men were doing in his country.

Major Rogers, impressed by the bold attitude of the Indian leader, politely replied that he and his Rangers were on their way to take over Fort Detroit in the name of the British Crown.

Pontiac's messengers had already told him of the whale boats beached on the shore. He knew of the Rangers and their search for a camp site.

Now he told Rogers sternly that he and his band of warriors would see that the invaders did not proceed until morning. He promised that he would at that time tell them whether or not they might go on to claim Detroit.

The chief asked if he could supply the Rangers with anything and then led his band back to his own camp, leaving the suspicious white men to stand guard all night.

The next morning Pontiac and his attendant chiefs came back with an answer for Rogers. Pontiac said he was willing to live in peace with the British and would let them stay in his country as long as they treated him with the respect due him

Pontiac Meets with Major Robert Rogers

as head chief. He conceded that he would call the British king "Uncle." After agreeing to this, Rogers smoked the calumet with Pontiac and his chiefs as a sign of friendship. Pontiac also promised to see that the Rogers party was not molested on the way to Detroit.

At this time Pontiac's attitude toward the British was one of "wait and see." However, whether as friend or foe, he did not intend to miss out on the ceremony of the surrender of Fort Detroit by the French, or on his part of the gifts that the English might pass out to the watching natives.

Many of the tribesmen around Detroit were in favor of having the post taken over by the British. They wanted to be with the winner and they had been promised that the British would provide better trading facilities for them at a lower cost than they had gotten from the French before and during the French and Indian War.

The English traders said they would fill the canoes of the hunters with blankets and kettles and knives and with beads of many colors, and the natives expected them to do just that. It sounded like a fine deal.

Few of the natives yet had any realization of what the surrender of the French territory in Canada would mean to them and to their way of life. At that time it did not seem important to them who claimed Fort Detroit, a really small section of land, as long as the white men and their guns and ammunition and goods were available for trade; and no one was concerned that the English believed the Indians were now living on British territory.

The Indians' relationship with the French, who had come into their country long before, had not involved any strict "mine and thine" of geography. They could not understand or foresee what they were letting themselves in for by accepting the change to British rule.

The report of the surrender of Canada and the coming change of the garrison at Detroit from French to British was regarded as good news by a small band of Ottawas who were English sympathizers and had moved from the Detroit area. They hinted to Pontiac and his followers that it was good to exchange their fathers, the French, for their brothers, the English, who might be more generous with gifts.

Early in November Pontiac received word from a runner that the Rangers were at the western end of Lake Erie and had halted there because of a scout's report to Rogers that a band of four hundred Indians was waiting in ambush along the river to attack the Rangers. Rogers reminded Pontiac of his promise to allow them safe passage to Detroit.

Pontiac hurried to the Detroit area to intercede for the Rogers party. He told the waiting warriors that it was foolish to fight after the French had surrendered. He pointed out that even if they killed Rogers and his men, more English soldiers with more guns would come.

"Make peace with the English," he urged. "The French do not fight them now. Why should you?"

As the Rogers boats resumed their journey to Fort Detroit, the leader sent a courier to Captain Beletre, the French commander of the fort, telling him of Canada's capitulation and advising him that an English force was on the way to replace the French garrison.

Beletre already knew of the surrender, but humiliated and angry over the defeat of Canada, he refused to accept the message and tried to arouse the Indians to aid him in resisting the take-over of the fort. However, this scheme did not work — the Indians, mindful of Pontiac's advice, seemed indifferent to the French commander's requests.

When Rogers' boats entered the mouth of the Detroit River, he could see the white houses of the Canadian farmers on each bank. The village of the Wyandots on the eastern shore and that of the Potawatomies on the west were almost opposite each other and beyond them on the western shore of the wide and deep Detroit River, was the palisaded fort, where the flag of France was flying for the last time.

The British landed on the opposite shore and pitched their tents.

On November 29, 1760, the surrender was carried out. Two British officers, with a small force of Royal Americans (a detachment of the Sixtieth Regiment) crossed the river to take possession.

Major Robert Rogers

While Pontiac and his men and several hundred other Indians of the area watched, Major Rogers and two hundred men of his force landed on a plain below the fort. The men drew up in ranks to await orders. Wearing their green buckskins and green Scottish caps, the Rangers made a deep impression on the natives, who were more familiar with the red coats of the British soldiers.

Major Rogers had brought along a company of regulars who were to form the garrison at Fort Detroit while he went on to take over and garrison the other surrendered forts.

Veteran Captain Donald Campbell, fat and near-sighted, but a brave and competent officer, was to take temporary charge of the fort.

Also accompanying Major Rogers was George Croghan,* an Irish trader and an agent of the British, whose mission was to hold council with the Indians and win them to the side of the British.

As the moment of surrender drew near, most of the Indians crowded up close to watch, but the French residents of the region, called "habitants," stood at a distance and tearfully awaited the take-over.

There was a deep hush of expectation as the gate of the fort opened and a French officer came out to extend the compliments of the commander, Captain Beletre, to Major Rogers.

Rogers ordered the British drums to beat while the two British officers and the Royal Americans marched in as if on dress parade. They proceeded to the center of the fort and stood stiffly at attention.

Pontiac, with folded arms and a stern look on his face, watched the small French garrison march out on the meadow.

The British drums beat sharply; the French garrison laid down their arms. The French fleur-de-lis flag was lowered from the flag staff and the British Cross of St. George was raised. The Indians greeted the red and white ensign with rousing yells. The Royal Americans added their cheers to the din of the natives.

Next the Canadian militia were called together and disarmed. This gesture of submission was viewed in amazement

---

* See Addenda at the end of the book for profiles on General Amherst, Major George Croghan, Major Henry Gladwyn and Sir William Johnson.

by Pontiac and his men. They stared in open-mouthed shock at seeing a live enemy lay down his arms without a shot being fired — an event unknown in the history of Indian warfare. They had no conception of the discipline imposed on royal troops in a so-called civilized war.

They recovered quickly, however, and joined with the others in shouts of approval at the colorful ceremony and the British show of strength. Privately all the natives wondered why the English soldiers did not destroy their former enemies. They had won, hadn't they?

When quiet was restored, the oath of allegiance to the British Crown was administered *en masse* to the French habitants and they were asked to give up their arms. The members of the French garrison were sent down the lakes as prisoners to be exchanged at Montreal. The habitants were allowed to retain their farms and homes.

Thus the old fort ended its life as a French post and became the English Fort Detroit.

Major Rogers left immediately, intending to lead a party up the lakes to Fort Michilimackinac at the north end of Lake Michigan, but the ice had already closed in. He was forced to abandon this project, leaving Michilimackinac and three other northern forts: Ste. Marie, Green Bay and St. Joseph, in French hands until the next season. The rugged major marched overland to Fort Pitt, reaching it on January 23, 1761. There his tour of duty ended.

George Croghan, in his role of conciliating the tribes in the Detroit area, held many councils with Pontiac and the other chiefs. He told the Indians that the French inhabitants of Detroit were now British subjects and painted a very rosy picture of the tribes having free and open trade with the English.

Croghan asked the Indians to turn their English prisoners, taken in raids on the settlements, over to him as a guarantee of friendship and of peaceful intentions. He also distributed small gifts to the natives along with the promises.

Pontiac had been an ally of the French during the time they occupied their forts, but now that the British had defeated them and taken over Canada, he believed that he must make friends with the new power to protect his people.

The Ottawa chief spent many hours pondering the situation. He wanted to believe that the English would keep their promises to share the land, but he had heard ugly rumors about the coldness and indifference of the British. His heart was heavy with responsibilities for his warriors who trusted him to guard their interests.

4

PONTIAC'S PLOT

As PONTIAC HAD FEARED, the country had barely been transferred to the English when there began to be complaints and mutters of dissatisfaction from the Indians. Discontent spread from lake to lake and to the rivers. Hatred for the "redcoats" soon became general among all the tribes.

The reasons for this are now easy to understand. The French, in the years of their association with the Indians, had offered them respect for their way of life and genuine friendship, and the tribes expected the same relationship with the English but it did not come about. The British forces, now firmly in power, treated the Indians with indifference and contempt, calling them nuisances and refusing to supply them with necessities such as ammunition and clothing. There were no presents and no hand-outs of food as promised.

Even the British fur-traders failed to maintain the free and easy camaraderie that the French bush-rangers and traders had shown.

Everything had changed, and nothing for the better, in the opinion of the Indians. Beside having their best hunting grounds taken over by the English, they saw new settlers moving in and surrounding their villages and camps. The white settlements seemed to spread like fire over the land to eat away at the forests and fields.

The Indians burned with desire to avenge the outrages against them, but they did not know how to plan a counter-plot to dislodge the invaders. Some of them did not fully realize the extent of the threat presented by the British take-over, but they felt uneasy and unhappy. They wanted the white man close enough so that they could enjoy his trade goods, rum and weapons, yet at the same time they wished to keep him hemmed in by Indian camps.

This could not be. Trying to hold back the onrush of white civilization was like trying to stop a giant wave that swept all before it.

Pontiac, fully alert to the English colonization movement, saw the almost inevitable end of his people and the Indian way of life. He held many conferences to alert the tribes to the true situation. He urged the natives to cease their war between the tribes and unite with their former enemies to fight the British in the common cause of retaining the land and the lakes that the Master-of-Life had created for his red children.

Far-sighted Pontiac was not long in sensing that even the united tribes could not defeat the English and their superior fire power. He decided that the Indians must help restore the French, who had been their friends and allies and had shared the country with them.

The Ottawa chief began on a plan to form a confedera-tion of Indians who would make war on the settlements, har-ass the English and then, in a general uprising, take over the surrendered forts one by one. So he dreamed.

Early in June of 1761, Captain Campbell, who was in command at Fort Detroit, sent messages to all the fort com-manders telling them that the Six Nations of the Iroquois had sent war belts of wampum to the Indian nations urging them to lift the hatchet against the English. He warned them that the Senecas, Delawares, and the Shawnees with other tribes from the north, planned to make a surprise attack on Niagara and Fort Pitt near the end of that month. This may have been the Iroquois' response to the projected action of their ancient enemies, the Algonquins. At any rate, the Ottawa chief did not join in it (he was not yet ready) and it came to nothing.

Some of the French traders and many inhabitants of the French settlements, smarting from their country's defeat, were anxious to stir up trouble by encouraging the Indians. In secret councils they told the natives that the English were determined to do away with every Indian. They said the tribes could see for themselves that the British had begun to hem them in with settlements on one hand and a chain of forts on the other.

The Canadians of French extraction told Pontiac that their French father, the king, was sending his armies to take back Canada. His soldiers, fighting alongside their Indian brothers, would certainly beat the English and drive them back to their original territory on the seacoast. At least that is what the Canadians said. Pontiac relayed the message to his warriors with fervent gestures and all the power of his eloquent tongue.

This appealing myth of the French king coming to their aid took such hold on the Indians, including Pontiac himself, that it was revived season after season to bolster the cause of war making. Whenever Pontiac spoke in council, he always alluded to the Indians' "French father" who would personally lead his armies across the lakes and aid the Indians in their fight to keep their tribal lands. The Ottawa chief never seemed to lose faith in this story until the last days of his life. Perhaps he wanted so badly for it to be true!

Adding to the turmoil, prophets that claimed to be messengers of the Great Spirit appeared among the tribes. Young men with blazing eyes and thundering tongues harangued the natives, urging them to return to the primitive life of their fathers. Then, the prophets promised, the Indians would be restored to their former greatness and be able to drive out the whites.

Pontiac listened as the young preachers stirred the superstitious Indians with fiery speeches about the need for living in the old way: using the bow and arrow instead of the white man's guns; wearing only skins for clothing, and giving up rum.

Formerly Pontiac had himself recommended a return to the old way of life, but now he realized that the young warriors were already too fond of the white soldier's firearms and tools to think of going back to the bow and arrow and the stone hatchet. Also they wanted no part of the buffalo hide wardrobe or the rumless life.

Pontiac learned that the Delawares, the Shawnees, the Senecas, and the Mohawks, whose lands had been invaded by English settlers without the Indians' knowledge or consent, were loudly protesting this outrage. When their complaints to the authorities fell on deaf ears, they voiced their grievances to any who would listen, but Pontiac had time only for his own plot. He worked tirelessly to perfect his confederation, planned his strategy in secret and then waited for the proper time to begin his campaign against the English.

Late in the year of 1762 Pontiac sent messengers to all the tribes in the Ohio country, the upper lakes regions, and south to the Indians along the Mississippi River. The wampum belt they carried was made long and wide, as befitted the importance of the word it carried. They also bore the red tomahawk, the war token, and showed it at every camp and village along their route. They summoned the head men of the tribes to assemble and hear the words of the great Chief Pontiac.

When they had gathered, the chief of the delegates stood

and flung the red tomahawk before them. Then, holding the war belt of wampum in his hands, he delivered word for word the speech Pontiac had given to him.

His vehement gestures and fiery words brought grunts of approval. The belt was ceremoniously taken from the messenger's hands, the hatchet was snatched up by the most honored warrior, and with these tokens of assent the chiefs of the tribes stood pledged to take part in Chief Pontiac's war against the British.

Pontiac set the date for a certain time in the month of May of the next year, according to the changes of the moon. All the tribes were to strike at or near the same day, each band destroying the English fort in its area. Then, in a mass assault, all were to attack the settlements of the frontier.

This carefully worked-out plan of Pontiac's was accepted by all the nations of the Algonquins, also by the Wyandots, the Senecas, and several tribes of the lower Mississippi. The Iroquois, with a few exceptions, did not join in the conspiracy.

While Pontiac was perfecting his great confederation, the new tenants of Fort Detroit proceeded to make themselves at home.

The men who lived in the area hunted, fished and traded. The country was fertile and the French farmers in the settlement grew their crops in narrow strips that extended for ten miles up and down the river. Neat and comfortable farm houses lined the shore where there was water for household use and also for traveling along the river in flat-bottomed boats called "bateaux."

Neighbors were close, and the fun-loving French habitants danced and dined and played cards in the evenings, went to church on Sunday and often joined the nearby Indians in games of lacrosse or in foot races and canoe races. Most of the

French could communicate with the natives in one or more Indian tongues.

In spite of hidden resentment over the loss of French territory, the habitants got along well with the English garrison of the fort and often entertained them in their homes. The farmers furnished the newcomers fresh vegetables, which were a welcome addition to the salt pork and beef the English troops received from Niagara. The Indians also brought in deer meat.

Captain Campbell wrote his superior officers that he was concerned about the four nations in the Detroit area: the Ottawas, Chippewas, Delawares and Potawatomies. He complained that they came to him for everything they wanted, but he had nothing to give them, not even small trifles such as the French had freely passed out to cement ties.

Pontiac often visited Captain Campbell at the fort. He urged the commander to request that English traders from Pittsburg be sent to Detroit.

English traders did come that spring and the natives had an opportunity to sell their winter catch of furs and to buy the things they wanted. However, the Indians protested that the traders' stocks contained mostly articles that only the French would want. They also objected to the high prices of the trade goods.

In order to keep a peaceful atmosphere at Fort Detroit, Captain Campbell asked his superiors to define regulations governing trade with the Indians. He needed to know how to supervise the traders' movements, how much to control prices, and how to limit the amount of rum sold. He also wanted credit terms clarified.

General Amherst,* commander-in-chief of the British forces in America, replied that to keep the Indians on friendly terms, the commanding officer at the fort should be empowered to supply them with small amounts of arms and ammu-

* See Addenda.

nition for hunting and a little clothing in cases of want. They were also to be given food for the journey home after visiting the fort. (Visiting the forts was a popular pastime with the Indians. They were fond of the white bread dotted with bits of English jam that the garrison passed out to them on leaving.) In turn the troops found this a convenient way to keep an eye on the natives.

In addition to these concessions, the British promised to provide a gunsmith to repair guns and utensils. There was already a doctor at the fort who had come out with the Rogers party the year before.

Sir William Johnson*, who was superintendent of the Northern Department and head of Indian affairs under Amherst, said the traders at Oswego (New York) made a fifty percent profit. He suggested that the traders at Detroit should have more because of the greater distance from the source of supply. He compiled a list of articles that the Indians wanted most.

On Johnson's list were blankets (in colors of blue, black and red), calicoes and ribbons, awls and needles and thread, scalping knives, vermillion (face and body paint), razors and scissors, iron and brass kettles, tobacco, tomahawks, black and white and red wampum, beaver traps and iron fish spears, and, most important of all, rum.

* See Addenda

General Sir Jeffrey Amherst

5

GENERAL AMHERST AND HIS INDIAN POLICY

GENERAL AMHERST CONSIDERED Captain Campbell too sympathetic to the Indian cause.

Shortly after sending his earlier directive, the general had a change of heart and began to tighten his orders in regard to the treatment of the Indians. He wanted clothing and ammunition given to the tribes only in case of dire necessity. He was not in favor of giving them food. He said if they found they could get supplies just by asking, they would neglect hunting and thereby destroy the profitable fur trade for the English. Also Amherst wished to keep the Indians busy foraging for food so they would have no time to hatch plots against the British.

He directed that no rum could be sold at the forts. This indignity (the cutting off of rum sales) was a sore point with the Indians and they protested bitterly against it but to no avail.

In addition, the Indians were now forced to bring their furs into the fort to sell them. They had been used to dealing with the French traders who came to the winter camps and spared them the task of hauling their catches to market.

Everything in the British regulations made the tribes more suspicious of the intentions of the new rulers and also more susceptible to Pontiac's stirring oratory and war talk.

The farsighted Ottawa leader coached his chiefs to say they would give up any prisoners (taken in raids on the settlements) who did not want to remain in their care. However, before yielding prisoners, the Indians wanted to have the price of trade goods lowered and firmly established at that figure, as had been promised. They reminded the British that their country had been given to them by the Master-of-Life and that the English had said they would preserve it for joint use by the Indians and themselves.

Pontiac dwelt on this matter in his speeches in council. He was determined to see the promise fulfilled.

Pontiac kept a close watch on the fort and attended the councils as an observer when he did not speak.

He learned that George Croghan had advised Sir William Johnson, General Amherst's chief deputy, that Indian affairs were not going as smoothly as expected, and that when Johnson visited the general in New York, a decision was made to send Johnson and Croghan to Detroit where they would hold a council with the Indians and resolve the difficulties.

General Amherst decided on a replacement for command of Fort Detroit. He also planned to send a sizable detachment of troops to enlarge the garrison at Forts Michilimackinac, Green Bay, St. Joseph, and the new post at Sandusky.

He ordered an expedition under command of Major Henry Gladwyn to relieve the Rangers at Fort Miamis and at Fort Ouatanon.

Major Gladwyn* was then thirty-two years old. He had served in the French and Indian War and had taken part in the surrender of Montreal in 1760.

Before taking command at Fort Detroit, Gladwyn's mis-

* See Addenda.

sion was to visit the surrendered posts and assign troops to maintain them. He and his regiment of two hundred men met Sir William Johnson at Niagara, where a conference was held while Sir William waited for his boats.

After the conference the Major went on to Detroit with his men, plus an additional sixty, with two officers from Niagara who would join Captain Campbell's garrison at Fort Detroit.

In August George Croghan arrived at Detroit, along with some Delaware chiefs he had picked up along the way.

Pontiac led a delegation of Ottawa chiefs to the meeting with Croghan. Wearing paint and feathers, bear-claw necklaces and armbands of fur and beads, and with scalps at their belts, the Indians entered the scene in grand style.

Croghan made some speeches to prepare the way for Sir William Johnson's council with the tribes later.

Some of the Delaware chiefs commended Pontiac and the Detroit natives for not accepting the Senecas' war belt and advised them to keep peace with the English.

Pontiac maintained his stately pose and made no reply.

In concluding the preparatory speeches, Croghan gave each nation of the Indians a keg of rum to warm them toward his cause.

After celebrating this important event with the gift of rum, Pontiac led his chiefs and warriors back to his camp.

In September Major Gladwyn reached Detroit in poor physical condition after a difficult voyage and took to his bed. Others of the party also stayed at Detroit to await the coming of Sir William Johnson.

When Johnson and his retinue arrived, they were royally entertained by the habitants. Captain Campbell also gave a dinner and a ball in honor of Sir William.

Pontiac let his curiosity get the better of his pride and joined the group of Indians watching outside Campbell's house for glimpses of the goings-on at the ball.

The natives viewed with amazement the gyrations of the dancing couples, the ladies in fancy gowns with bare, bejeweled necks, and the British officers in their uniforms bedecked with brilliant decorations.

It was not the kind of dancing Pontiac and the others were used to seeing.

The Ottawa chief and his men attended Johnson's grand council which was held out of doors on September 9. He and the other chiefs and warriors wore their finest and most colorful regalia with headdresses of feathers and buffalo horns and with scalps swinging at their belts.

After the ceremonial greeting the pipe was passed, wampum strings exchanged, and then the speeches began. In Indian councils, protocol demanded that the party calling the council speak first and be allowed to have his say without interruption.

When all the speeches from one side had been heard, the conference would break up until the next day.

Johnson, in his speech, said that he was acting for their English father in declaring peace between the Indians and the British. He told the natives that King George was attentive to the needs of all his children and assured them of his favor to all who were willing to enter an alliance with the British. He said the Indians would be deprived only of land necessary for promoting commerce benefiting them, or land to which the British had legal claims. He scolded them for not having turned in all their captives.

What Johnson did not tell the Indians was that en route to Detroit he had received a message from General Amherst.

The message ordered him to refrain from giving presents to the Indians so they would work harder to obtain food and thus would have less time to plot against the English. Amherst also told Johnson to keep the tribes short of ammunition so they would not be able to attack the garrison.

Sir William Johnson was well aware of the adverse effect

these orders would have on the natives, so he did not mention them.

After Johnson had finished speaking, one of the Mohawks who had accompanied the Johnson party to Detroit spoke of the advantages of being an ally of the British. He warned the other tribes to pay no attention to rumors carried by the other Iroquois nations, namely the Senecas, because the Mohawks lived closest to the English (Sir William Johnson had married a Mohawk girl) and would be the first to know of moves by the British.

Next day the Detroit tribes replied. A Huron chief pledged that his nation would be faithful friends of the English. He said all captives had been turned over to Croghan. He then urged Johnson to make good his promises about trade goods because so far the natives had found goods too high in price and ammunition so scarce as to hinder them in hunting. As he spoke he presented a wampum belt for each point in his speech.

At the close of the Huron's speech, Chief Mecatepilesis rose to speak for the Ottawa federation of four bands — the Suskatoons, Sinagoes, Sables and Massauaketons. He said that his nation had begun to look upon the English as friends. He handed over a belt of wampum and went on to say that his people were pleased with Johnson's words and would act in agreement with them. Giving another belt, he said that "bad birds" among them had set his people against their brothers, the English, but henceforth they would pay no attention to such disturbers but would hold fast to the chain of peace. The "bad birds" expression was often used by the Indians when attempting to shift the blame for misbehaving.

Mecatepilesis finished his speech and offered another belt. He then turned to the Mohawks and assured them there was no longer ill will between them and the Ottawa confederation of four over an old quarrel. He gave the Mohawks a bunch of black and white wampum and sat down.

A Chippewa chief spoke next, after which Johnson concluded the conference. He passed out the gifts he had brought along and ordered an ox to be roasted for the Indians to feast upon. "Feed them and win them" was his strategy.

Sir William extended his stay in Detroit and held private meetings with some of the chiefs, including Pontiac. He was more sympathetic to the Indians' cause than the other white men in command and spent part of the time in drawing up rules and regulations for trade and in writing instructions for the fort commanders.

According to the regulations the pelts the Indians brought in were rated in line with the scale of exchange used at Forts Miamis, Pitt and Sandusky.

In trade, a "stroud," described as a small blanket of coarse texture, cost three beavers or four buckskins. A single striped blanket cost two beavers; a pound of gunpowder, one beaver. The price of a man's shirt was one beaver; a ruffled shirt cost two beaver pelts.

Before leaving Fort Detroit, Johnson ordered its officers to maintain good relations with the Indians in the area and to keep in touch with the commanders at other forts so they could act in unison if necessary. He wanted them to employ an interpreter. He told them to see that the natives obeyed the regulations. He said to allow the Indians the services of the gunsmith at the expense of the British. He did *not* go into the matter of giving presents or ammunition, nor did he mention rum.

On leaving the fort Johnson held a meeting at the Huron village across the river from Detroit. At that conference, a chief asked that the English traders sell the Indians goods on credit, to be paid for after the furs were brought in, as the French had done. He also requested that they be given some hoes so the squaws could cultivate their corn patches that had been allowed to go idle. It is probable that Pontiac had advised him to make a point of this since the Ottawa chief knew the

Sir William Johnson

Hurons were as short of ammunition and food as were his own people. Pontiac could see the shadow of hunger and want beginning to cover the Indian land.

Sir William Johnson reported to General Amherst that prospects for peace with the natives were good. He gave the general some information about the census of Indians in Detroit and Saginaw Bay areas. He said there were 1,180 (220 of them Ottawas) in an alliance with the Delawares, Shawnees, Miamis, Weas, Mascoutons, Kickapoos and other nations of the north. He told Amherst that the Indians showed no antagonism toward the garrisons at the forts but became suspicious of reinforcements or of new forts, like the one being built at Sandusky.

Pontiac asked why the English needed many forts. He said, "We have our canoes. We can come to them when we want to trade."

General Amherst advised Johnson that he wanted a blockhouse at Sandusky to keep up communications and also to keep the Canadians in line. He insisted on having it. As for the Indians, he believed the Detroit area would remain quiet because there was no chance of the Indians being irritated by any British action. He had little idea of the real situation.

As the British authorities talked peace, Pontiac was giving eloquent voice to complaints against them. He called the British liars and said they were demanding a higher price in furs for their trade goods than had been settled on at Fort Pitt — selling a blanket for three beavers instead of two and putting the ratio at six raccoons for one beaver.

Pontiac also resented the ban on the sale of rum at the forts. His warriors had grown very fond of the white man's firewater.

Another project the Ottawa chief wanted to set up was a yearly gathering of Indians and British. This idea was popular with all the tribes. Gatherings and conferences with the white men meant gifts for the Indians, which in their opinion could not be overdone. They considered it a sort of rental for the use of their land during the period it was being occupied. It did not occur to them that it was a permanent arrangement.

When Captain Campbell learned about General Amherst's orders to keep the tribes short of ammunition, he wrote to the other commanders, suggesting that if the Indians knew about the orders, they might cause trouble. However, later in the year he wrote to Fort Pitt saying that the natives had gone to the hunting grounds and would not be heard from again until spring. He said he hoped the general would change his attitude in regard to Indian affairs.

Captain Campbell thought if the tribes were allowed more powder and lead, it would keep them quiet and peaceable.

While the British were setting up a scheme for controlling the natives, Pontiac was busy with his own plans, keeping out of the spotlight and waiting for the proper time to launch his campaign for dislodging the British. He was fully convinced that his grand conspiracy would succeed and that he, as head chief of the confederation, would take the commander's place at Fort Detroit.

6

THE INDIANS RESENT
ENGLISH RULE

PONTIAC'S MEN in their swift canoes brought word to him from all the lakes region. They told him of every move the English made. In addition the contents of letters and messages from fort commanders to their headquarters often were spilled to the chief by French employees, traders and others.

He learned that Sir William Johnson had written to General Amherst saying he considered it necessary to supply the commanding officers at Oswego, Niagara and Detroit with clothing, ammunition and other articles to be given to deserving Indians who had been accustomed to receiving presents in abundance. Johnson said he wondered if it was wise to cut off all this until everything had been settled and peace firmly established throughout the country.

General Amherst, in his powdered wig and gold braid, sat in his comfortable headquarters and replied that his orders about no presents to the Indians were to be strictly obeyed. No exceptions could be made.

Amherst called the Indians savages and nuisances. He said they, and particularly Pontiac, must be gotten rid of by some means.

General Amherst sent an expedition under Captain Balfour to garrison Fort Michilimackinac, which had been abandoned by its French commander, Captain Louis de Beaujeu, in the fall of 1760. This far-north fort in the area where Pontiac was born and had spent his boyhood, was smaller than Fort Detroit and less crowded on the inside. It was the most important post north of Detroit for trading and other commerce on the lakes.

Several Indian tribes used Michilimackinac as a vacation spot. Chippewas lived nearby, and a large village of Ottawas was located on Lake Michigan, a few miles to the southwest. Some half-breed traders occupied the fort as headquarters under the command of Lieutenant Charles de Langlade, who was also a trader and had been a French officer in the late war. Langlade was authorized to transfer the fort to Captain Balfour. A few English traders had already ventured into the area to gather trade from the tribes. Amherst considered British troops were needed there for both business and military security. Too, he wanted to make a clean sweep of clearing the French soldiers from the forts.

After furnishing Michilimackinac with a garrison, Captain Balfour supplied the abandoned fort of La Baye at the head of Green Bay with a garrison of seventeen men commanded by Ensign James Gorrell. He next went south to Fort St. Joseph on the St. Joseph River. This fort had been abandoned by its French garrison some time before. Ensign Francis Schlosser and fifteen men were left there.

Balfour and the remaining men of the expedition returned to Detroit overland.

Pontiac knew of these replacements almost as soon as they were made. His amazement grew as he learned of beardless young English officers being placed in command of the forts. These small and sparsely manned posts, set at widely separated points in a vast expanse of forest and water, were surrounded by Indians — some apparently friendly, others openly hostile but all ready to take the warpath on short notice.

The chief stored these facts in his mind. They would be useful to him later.

Many of the British troops in America were young adventurers who were out to see the New World and the Indians as well as to gain fame and fortune while serving His Majesty, the King of England. Their officers were young also, and often inexperienced in Indian warfare.

Assignment to a lonely isolated post surounded by bands of savages often meant capture, torture and death to the commander as well as to the garrison. However, England was suffering a depression at that time and many young fellows wanted to have a go at America.

Pontiac had advised his allies to keep close watch on the British at Detroit and their moves were reported to him daily. In addition, messengers brought news from camps and villages hundreds of miles away. News of the forts being supplied with garrisons was disturbing to the Ottawa chief, but he kept his own counsel and continued planning his campaign.

There were changes at Fort Detroit in October, 1762.

Gladwyn recovered from the illness that had kept him in bed since his arrival at Detroit, became able to travel, and in October returned to Fort Edward Augustus. He would later be reassigned to Fort Detroit.

The rest of Gladwyn's force returned to Niagara to forward provisions to Detroit.

The new blockhouse at Sundusky that Amherst had insisted must be built, was finished in November, 1762. Its builder, Lieutenant Elias Meyer, was put in command of it and of a garrison of fifteen men.

With these moves the British had taken over and garrisoned all the former French forts among the western Great Lakes.

At this point even the dullest of the Detroit Indians began to realize the true meaning of General Amherst's policy toward them and to feel its disastrous effect.

Pontiac held councils with the chiefs and bitterly pointed out the facts of the new regime.

When the hunters returned to their villages with the furs they had taken during the winter, there was no rum available for the celebration they had customarily held when the French occupied the forts. The natives had used up all their ammunition and could get only handfuls. They received barely enough to use for shooting game to feed their families during the summer.

The Indians remembered the old days with the generous French and were resentful of the new British regulations.

Captain Campbell tried smoothing this antagonism over with speeches and small gifts of tobacco, rum and powder.

The French habitants spread rumors that Spain had joined France as an ally (Britain had declared war on Spain January 2, 1762) and that the French and Spaniards were on their way to retake Quebec. This kept the Indians stirred up and gave them a new spirit of independence.

As a matter of record, France and Great Britain were still at war in spite of the surrender of Canada. Spain had come into the war on France's side and France still held Louisiana, including the forts on the Mississippi and the one at Vincennes on the Wabash River.

The French settlers tried to promote the idea that France could rout the English and recover Canada. They enlarged on the story that a new French expedition was on its way to recapture Quebec and Montreal.

Even Pontiac, intelligent and farseeing though he was,

stoutly believed in this attractive fairy tale. Neither he nor any others of the Indians had the slightest idea of European politics and affairs, and their mind-picture of the King of France arriving in a great fleet of ships to aid the Indians was one they could not resist.

The French habitants continued to talk of how the British were plotting to do away with the natives. First, they warned, the British would cut off supplies of ammunition so the Indians could not defend themselves. Already, they suggested, the tribes could see the working of this plan. Were they not now being kept short of powder and lead?

At Fort Detroit, while Pontiac built up his confederation of chiefs and warriors, Captain Campbell was busy getting provisions for his own post and for the dependent ones. On June 4th, King George's birthday, Campbell gave a ball for the habitants of the fort. All was pleasant on the surface and the natives showed respect for the veteran commander.

General Amherst, the master strategist who liked to keep his officers moving, sent Major Henry Gladwyn to command Fort Detroit. Gladwyn arrived at the fort August 23, 1762, along with several officers and another company of Royal Americans. Captain Campbell was supposed to go to the fort on St. Mary's River but Major Gladwyn wished to keep the captain as his second-in-command. Also kept at Detroit was Lieutenant Hay.

It was a lonely life for the British troops and their commanders, guarding the isolated posts and keeping the natives on peaceful terms. That was why General Amherst believed his officers needed a frequent change of scenery.

While Gladwyn had a peaceful year at Detroit, Pontiac worked on his plan to oust the English. The chief held a secret council with the civil chiefs and the war chiefs of the Ottawas, Chippewas, Hurons, Potawatomies, and of the Lake Superior tribes who had with them two Frenchmen dressed as Indians.

This secret council was reported by an Ottawa Indian to George Croghan, the trader.

The informer did not know what was discussed in the council but he was certain it was a plot against the British. What he was sure of was that messengers were sent to carry news of the council's decision to the tribes on the Wabash and to the Shawnees in the Ohio Valley.

Nothing of Pontiac's secret council was leaked to the other Indians, even those around Detroit.

Croghan, alarmed at the news of this plot, talked to some trusted Iroquois who said they had heard the same rumors from a Shawnee brave. This upset Croghan and he sent word to Johnson and General Amherst.

The general said he was not concerned about the report. He had ordered a reduction in the expense and personnel of Johnson's Indian Department, cutting off the presents that Croghan had been giving to the Indians. Evidently the general could not believe that his tightwad policy would infuriate the Indians enough for them to cause trouble.

Pontiac, after his secret council, redoubled his efforts to stir up the tribes and bring them into his confederation. In a short time he had become the leader of all those Indians who disliked the British and wanted the French to rule.

In December, 1762, one of Croghan's traders returned from a trip to the Shawnees and reported that the tribe had received a war belt and hatchet from the Weas on the Wabash River that spring. The agent warned that the tribes believed the British were preparing to annihilate all the Indians as soon as their white captives were released.

He said the natives had expected all their wants to be supplied by the English and that they were now bitterly disappointed as well as in dire distress. This agent warned that cutting off the presents and denying ammunition was resented by all the tribes. He thought a general war might result.

At that time, actually, the only thing that prevented a

Major George Croghan

widespread uprising was the lack of an Indian leader strong
enough and popular enough to weld into one the various fac-
tions who were so often jealous and suspicious of one another.
Pontiac was building his confederation but he was not ready to
declare war.

In the Ohio valley new Indian "prophets" appeared to
speak of their visions. They gained many converts. Groups of
Indians traveled far to hear them describe the visions and
preach their doctrine of self-dependence.

Pontiac had long been aware of the prophets' powerful
appeal to the natives. He himself had once advocated a return
to the simple life of their forefathers, but he was wise enough
to know that the time for such a return was long past.

With Pontiac spreading his resentment and dissatisfaction
and preaching revenge throughout the Lakes area, the troubles
between the British and the Indians grew more ominous. Amherst's orders to allow only dribbles of ammunition to the natives was like taking food from their mouths. Nor were the
trade goods priced as low as had been promised. Also there
were no presents even when prisoners were returned.

However, the lack of rum was the main cause of the

tribes' anger and resentment. When the forts were in French hands, the young braves had been given plenty of rum to secure their allegiance.

By this time General Amherst had had his fill of the rugged life in the New World. He was awaiting word that he could return to England and the world of culture, snuff boxes and tea. He refused to change his position on the treatment of the Indians.

With Canada surrendered and peace in sight, Amherst could see no benefit from appeasing the natives at the expense of the Crown. He gave orders forbidding the soldiers to mingle with the tribes. He said he wanted no Indians visiting in the forts. Savages, as he called them, were expected to state their business and leave promptly. These strict regulations were in sad contrast with the free and easy friendliness of the French settlers and traders whom the Indians had known for years. Visiting the forts had been a popular pastime with the natives. They sadly missed the contacts with the white men and the small gifts that had been handed out at the forts.

The Delawares and the Iroquois to the east had thought the English would force out the French soldiers and restore the hunting grounds to them. But after the English drove out the French military, the English themselves stayed. In addition new settlers had poured into the valleys and built homes on the creeks and rivers. The Senecas complained about surrendering a native, accused of murdering a white man, to be tried by English law.

The Great Lakes tribes viewed the problem of the growing number of settlers with much alarm.

Pontiac, speaking in council, complained bitterly that the English swarmed on the lakes like mosquitoes in the swamps. He declared that the English were growing stronger with each year and the tribes must drive them out before they entirely possessed the land.

7

PONTIAC REVEALS HIS PLOT
TO HIS WARRIORS

AT THE END of 1762 Pontiac sent messengers to the various tribes. By canoe and by foot they went to the country of the Ohio and its tributaries, north to the upper lakes region and the Ottawa River, and far to the south toward the mouth of the Mississippi. They carried the war belt of wampum, made long and wide as the importance of the message called for, and the red tomahawk of war. As they went from camp to camp and from village to village, their appearance was a signal for the chiefs and head men to gather and listen to the words brought to them from the great Chief Pontiac.

Early in the next year, the commanders of the far-flung forts began to notice the restlessness of the tribes and wrote to each other about their concern over this.

Ensign Holmes, commanding at Fort Miamis, reported to Major Gladwyn at Detroit as follows:

"Since my last letter to you wherein I acquainted you of the bloody belt (war belt) being in this village, I have made all the search I could about it, and have found it to be true; whereon I assembled all the chiefs of this nation and after a long and troublesome spell with them, I ob-

tained the belt, with a speech, as you will receive enclosed; This affair is very timely stopt (sic) and I hope
the news of a peace will put a stop to any further troubles with these Indians, who are the principal ones of
setting mischief on foot. I send you the belt with this
packet, which I hope you will forward to the General."*

The spring season of 1763 saw Pontiac agitating and
stirring up war spirit both in his own village and among the
neighboring tribes. He had completed his plot and was ready
to begin the war. His messengers had gone out even to the
hunting camps in the north woods urging chiefs and warriors
to attend the general council on the banks of the Ecorse River
(near Detroit) where he was camped.

Pontiac, with his squaws and children, greeted the bands
of Indians as they landed and set up their wigwams. It took
several days for them all to assemble. The council began April
27, 1763. Early in the morning the heralds of the camp ran
among the lodges, calling the warriors to the meeting.

When they had gathered and had seated themselves in
rows on the grass, the pipe was passed from hand to hand
while they waited in silence for the speaker, Pontiac, to appear.

When Pontiac, commanding in appearance and wearing
the full regalia of war paint and feathers, stepped into the midst
of the council circle, a prolonged grunt of approval came from
the assembly.

There were Chippewas with quivers of arrows slung on
their backs and war-clubs in their arms, Ottawas wearing
gaudy blankets over naked bodies, and Wyandots, also called
Hurons (French for *bristle head*) with their fierce looking
hair roaches and war paint. Many had scalps hanging from
their belts — all giving the meeting a wild and ferocious appearance.

The Ottawa chief looked about at the faces and began his
speech in his usual powerful and eloquent style. When he

* All quoted material in this book is from *The Conspiracy of Pontiac* by Francis Parkman. Courtesy: Little, Brown & Co. Publishers,
Boston, Mass., 1901.

paused, the Indians gave grunts of assent and urged him on to relate the injustices they had suffered at the hands of the English. He told of the treatment that could be expected if the English remained in power — that they had driven out the French and undoubtedly were only waiting for a chance to get rid of the Indians.

Then Pontiac held out a wide and handsome belt of wampum, and told the Indians that their father, the great king of France, had sent it. He said the king had heard the prayers of his red children and now his great canoes filled with soldiers were ready to sail up the St. Lawrence River and win back his dominion in Canada.

The Ottawa chief thought this falsehood about receiving the wampum belt necessary to accomplish his purpose in arousing the Indians to resist the British take-over. He fervently wished it might come true — that he would receive such a war belt.

Stirred by the war talk and chance for revenge, the Indians loudly cheered the chief and yelled their consent.

Pontiac, delighted to find so much loyalty among the more than four hundred Indians present, decided to hold his listeners while he related a long story of mystery and superstition designed to enhance their tribal spirit.

In this tale, a Delaware Indian (the French called them *Loups* meaning *wolves*, but their own name for the tribe was *Lenni Lenape*, meaning *Original Man*) set out to learn wisdom from the Master-of-Life. Since he did not know where to find him, the Delaware encountered many adventures before he stood at last before the Great Spirit and gazed astounded at the magnificence of his surroundings.

The Master-of-Life bade the Delaware pilgrim be seated and then spoke to him as follows:

"I am the Maker of heaven and earth, the trees, lakes, rivers and all things else. I am the Maker of mankind; and because I love you, you must do my will. The land on which you live I have made for you and not for others. Why do you suffer the white men to dwell among you? My children, you have forgotten the customs and traditions of your forefathers. Why do you not clothe yourselves in skins, as they did, and use the bows and arrows, and the stone-pointed lances, which they used? You have bought guns, knives, kettles, and blankets from the white men until you can no longer do without them; and, what is worse, you have drunk the poison firewater which turns you into fools.

"Fling all these things away; live as your wise forefathers lived before you. And as for these English — these dogs dressed in red, who have come to rob you of your hunting-grounds and drive away the game — you must lift the hatchet against them. Wipe them from the face of the earth, and then you will win my favor back again, and once more be happy and prosperous. The children of your great father, the king of France, are not like the English. Never forget that they are your brethren. They are very dear to me, for they love the red man and understand the true mode of worshipping me."

The Great Spirit next gave his hearer various precepts of morality and religion, such as the prohibition to marry more than one wife; and a warning against the practice of magic, which is worshipping the devil. A prayer, embodying the substance of all that he had heard was then presented to the Delaware. It was cut in hieroglyphics upon a wooden stick, after the custom of his people; and he was directed to send copies of it to all the Indian villages.

At the end of the discourse, which called for ridding the land of the English, the crafty Pontiac again managed to insert some propaganda for the French by saying that the celestial being urged the Delaware to remain friends with his brethren, the French, who were very dear to him.

As Pontiac finished his tale, he saw every man in the council aroused and eager to attack the fort at Detroit.

He then told them details of the plan he had kept secret for so long.

While they waited in hushed expectation, he said that on May 1st, he would visit the fort. On pretense of dancing the calumet dance before the garrison, he and a party of his warriors would spy out the situation inside and take note of the strength of the fortification. He would then call another meeting to decide on the exact mode of attack.

Pontiac dissolved the council then, and with his precious secret in their minds and hearts, the natives departed for their homes.

The women loaded the canoes that had been drawn up on the river bank, and by sunrise the entire assembly had vanished. Everything looked as usual, with the Indian natives in the Detroit area lounging about the fort and asking for gifts as was their custom.

In accordance with his promise to the tribesmen, Pontiac did appear at the gates of the fort on May 1st, with forty of his Ottawas. He asked permission to enter and dance the calumet dance before the officers of the garrison. There was some question as to whether the Indians should be permitted to enter, but finally they were let inside. Pontiac and thirty of his men danced the ritual of the calumet dance before a group of officers and men while the remaining ten Ottawas strolled about and spied the layout. When the dance was over, Pontiac took his warriors and left without arousing any suspicion.

After a few days Pontiac sent his messengers to call another council of chiefs. This time it was held in the Potawatomie village.

The council house, a huge bark lodge, was filled with a hundred chiefs sitting in a circle while the pipe was passed from hand to hand.

Pontiac entered and stood outlined in the light of the council fire. Bold and commanding, he looked a true leader.

He stirred the smokers with his oratory before giving them the details of his plan of battle. He thundered that the Master-of-Life had commanded his red children to drive the English from their land!

After the din of encouraging yells had ceased, he said he would demand a council with the commander on important matters, so that he and his principal chiefs would be admitted within the fort. They would all carry weapons concealed beneath their blankets. Then, while he was speaking to the commander in the council room, he would signal with a wampum belt for the other chiefs to raise the war whoop and make a sudden, fierce attack on the officers of the fort. As soon as the yells and noise of the battle in the council room were heard, the Indians waiting at the gate were to rush upon the surprised, half-armed soldiers, strike them down and take possession of the fort. He assured his listeners that the English had hearts like old women.

Pontiac knew well the pride and independence of his followers so he did not *order* them to follow his plan. He only counseled and inspired them. But his power and influence were so great that no questions were asked and no one opposed his plan. Loud grunts of approval followed his speech.

The chiefs gathered their blankets about them and headed for their own villages to begin preparations for the taking of the garrison at Fort Detroit.

The most important task was filing off gun barrels so the weapons would not show beneath their blankets.

8

THE CHIEF SUFFERS
A CRUSHING BLOW

PONTIAC CALLED HIS final council at the Potawatomie village
two miles below the fort on the north side of the river. Secrecy
was demanded. *All was hush-hush*. The date set: May 5, 1763.
As an extra precaution he ordered that no women be allowed
to attend the council or to remain in the village during the time
of conference.

When the chiefs and warriors were assembled and the
pipe had been passed, Pontiac rose and again recited a list of
grievances that the Indians most resented.

After receiving grunts of approval, Pontiac launched into
his sales talk to induce the tribesmen to attack the English.

He taunted them: "The other nations are attacking the
English. Why do we wait?" He reminded them that the
French could not protect the English even if they wished to
do so, because their arms had been surrendered. He urged the
Indians with all his powerful oratory, to lift the hatchet
against the English, drive them back to the eastern coast and
into the sea. Then he told them that he had sent wampum
belts to the Chippewas of Saginaw, the Ottawas of Michili-

mackinac, and the Ottawas of Thames River to the east. He vowed that these tribes would join in the war, and he wound up his speech with a fiery appeal to strike at once.

The Indians gave a tumultuous roar of approval to Pontiac's speech. Then they settled down to listen while he outlined his specific plot against Fort Detroit.

Pontiac's plan was to enter the fort on the second day after this meeting and ask Gladwyn for a council. Accompanying him there would be sixty seasoned warriors (actually there were forty) carrying tomahawks, knives and sawed-off muskets under their blankets. The rest of the Ottawas, men and women, also carrying concealed weapons, were to crowd through the gate into the fort and take places around the enclosure. At a signal from Pontiac they were to lift the hatchet and strike the unsuspecting English soldiers of the garrison.

Pontiac's plan left it to the Hurons to divide forces. While one band circled the fort at a distance (aiming to capture the persons who worked outside the fort) the other band would patrol the Detroit River to stop any English reinforcements or approaching vessel.

On the morning of May 7, 1763 Pontiac gathered his chiefs and warriors and crossed the river. The squaws followed in their canoes.

Pontiac, in full regalia of paint and feathers and ornaments of bear claws, with three hundred braves behind him, stalked through the gate and past the sentries (double the usual number) who stood with fixed bayonets. The crowd pushed in after their chief and his men and gathered in small groups about the buildings inside.

Pontiac headed for Captain Campbell's house, the site of the council. His mind was full of questions — the extra sentinels at the gate and their fixed bayonets — the closed shops — the soldiers armed and drawn up on the parade ground. All these were bad omens!

Inside the council room Pontiac suffered a shattering blow. He almost reeled when he saw that Major Gladwyn and Captain Campbell wore their side arms. The interpreters were beside them but the other officers were dispersed among the garrison and stood close to the gate.

These things alerted Pontiac and his ten chiefs to the fact that the English were aware of his plot and had prepared to defend themselves.

It was a cruel setback but the stout-hearted Pontiac was able to keep his composure. The warriors, aware that something had gone terribly wrong, showed their anxiety by shifting their feet and fixing their eyes on their leader. Finally, at an imperious gesture from the chief, they sat down in gingerly fashion and waited for him to speak.

Pontiac's first words were spoken boldly, "Why do I see our father's young men with their arms?" He went on to say that perhaps some "bad bird" had told evil tales about the tribes. He advised Gladwyn and his officers not to believe these tales because the Indians had always been good friends of the English.

Gladwyn's reply was that he was expecting some other Indian nations to visit him and wanted to be prepared when they came. He slyly added that he was sure his friends, the Ottawas, would not misunderstand his action.

Pontiac calmly accepted this untruth because he could not openly dispute the commander.

The chief then rose to his feet, holding a wampum belt in his hands, and said that he had come to smoke the pipe of peace and brighten the chain of friendship.

Just as he started to lift the belt in reverse (which was the pre-arranged signal for the attack to begin) a sudden, thunderous roll of drums calling for the charge filled the room.

Pontiac, startled, let his arm fall and stood perplexed, not knowing what to expect. Forced to make a lightning change of plan, since his chance of surprising the garrison was gone, he sat down and waited for Gladwyn to speak.

Briefly the commander told Pontiac and the chiefs that friendship would be extended to them as long as they deserved it. He added that any aggressive act would be revenged.

Pontiac then broke up the council. Before leaving he told Major Gladwyn that he would return in a few days with his wives and children. He wished that they should shake hands with their fathers, the English.

Gladwyn made no reply to this statement and Pontiac led his chiefs in a stately file out the gates of the fort.

The Ottawa chief's elaborate precautions to keep his plot a secret had gone for nothing for various reasons. A few of the Indians were lukewarm toward the plan — some had friends among the English garrison or the traders.

Another factor was that a secret of such importance could not be kept for two days. Gladwyn knew of the plot the night before it was to be carried out.

Note: There are many versons of this fateful incident. Major Gladwyn wrote his own interpretation of it to his superior officer, General Amherst. In a letter dated May 14, 1763, he said:

"Sir:

On the first instant, the chief of the Ottawa nations, came here with about fifty of his men (forty) and told me that in a few days when the rest of his nation came in (from hunting) he intended to pay me a formal visit. The 7th he came, but I was luckily informed, the night before, that he was coming with an intention to surprise us: upon which I took such precautions that when they entered the fort (tho they were, by the best accounts, about three hundred, and armed with knives, tomyhawks, and a great many with guns cut short, and hid under their blankets,) they were so much surprised to see our disposition, that they could hardly sit down to council. However, in about half an hour, after they saw their designs were discovered, they sat down and Pontiac made a

speech which I answered calmly, without intimating my
suspicion of their intentions, and after receving some
trifling presents, they went away to their camp."

As they stalked away from the fort area, the chiefs were
silent, reflecting Pontiac's mood of frustration and anger. The
other Indians were furious and more than a little baffled at the
turn of events. All returned to the Ottawa village.

Pontiac met in council with the chiefs as soon as they arrived at the camp. They rebuked him for failing to give the
signal to attack, inquiring why he did not give the signal for
the lifting of the war hatchet.

Pontiac, his face livid with rage and disappointment, replied in tones of bitter reproach. He asked if they had not seen
that Gladwyn's young men had their arms with them. He said
he would not make war on an enemy who was ready and prepared: he would not risk the lives of his warriors.

The chief paused to let his words sink in, then added,
"Now I have thought of a way to give you another chance
at the English. I will speak of it in the full council."

Then Pontiac posed the question: "What *bad bird* told
Gladwyn of the intended attack?"

Suspicion was directed to a pretty young Chippewa
squaw, named Catherine, who lived in the Potawatomie village.
She had visited the fort the day before to deliver a pair of
moccasins she had made for Major Gladwyn. The girl was
known to be an admirer of the handsome young commander
and this was reason enough to suspect her.

Pontiac sent four warriors to cross the river and seize the
girl. Trembling and tearful, she was taken into the fort to face
the commander, while the men questioned her. Major Gladwyn refused to say it was she who had given him the news of
the plot. In spite of the girl's protestations of innocense, the
four Indians then took her to Pontiac, who sentenced her to a
flogging for her disloyalty.

"The Conspiracy of Pontiac Revealed

Another report of the incident gives the following details:
On the afternoon of May 6, Catherine entered the fort
and took to Major Gladwyn's quarters a pair of elk-hide moccasins ornamented with porcupine quills that he had requested
her to make for him. She appeared sad and downcast and soon
left the room. Later the sentinel saw her lingering inside the

to Major Gladwyn by an Indian Girl"

fort, although it was nearly time for closing the gates. The commander asked her why she had not left the fort before closing time. Catherine was reluctant to speak but after being urged to do so, she exacted a promise that the major would not betray her and then told him her secret.

"Tomorrow," she said, "Pontiac will come to the fort

with sixty of his chiefs. Each will be armed with a gun, cut short and hidden under his blanket. Pontiac will demand to hold a council, and after he has delivered his speech, he will offer a peace-belt of wampum, holding it in a reverse position. This will be the signal of attack. The chiefs will spring up and fire upon the officers, and the Indians in the street (of the fort) will fall upon the garrison. Every Englishman will be killed, but not the scalp of a single Frenchman will be touched."

Another version of the betrayal says that a French house-wife went to the Indian camp to buy deer meat and saw the braves filing their gun barrels to short lengths so the weapons could be hidden under their blankets. There are variations of both stories — perhaps it *was* the "bad birds" who warned Gladwyn of Pontiac's plot.

Before breaking up the council, Pontiac told his disap-pointed warriors that he would go to the fort on the next day and convince the commander he had been mistaken about the Ottawas intending to do harm.

Then the chief said when suspicion had been allayed, the fort could be taken by another surprise attack.

Early the next morning Pontiac and three of his chiefs went to the fort on their mission of erasing suspicion from the mind of the commander. When they were admitted to talk with him, the Ottawa chief offered the sacred calumet and said:

"My fathers, evil birds have sung lies into your ears. We that stand before you are friends of the English. We love them as our brothers, and, to prove our love, we have come this day to smoke the pipe of peace."

Pontiac added that he and his young men, some of them

not yet back from the hunting grounds, would come the next day to smoke the peace pipe and shake the commander's hand, thus assuring him that his suspicions were unjustified.

Major accepted the calumet and replied, "I have no business with the young men. Only chiefs may sit in council and there is no occasion for the young braves to visit me."

Pontiac felt that he had accomplished his mission and went back to his camp. That afternoon he decided to give the English more assurance that he had only friendship on his mind. He started a game of ball (lacrosse) on the nearby field. During the noise and excitement of the game, in which most of the young Indians took part, Pontiac visited the Potawatamie village and held council with the chiefs of that tribe and of the Wyandots about ways to dispose of the English.

On May 9, Pontiac, at the head of a large gathering of Indians, went to the fort. He found the gate (usually open during daylight hours) closed and barred.

The chief shouted to the guards, demanding to know why he was locked out.

Major Gladwyn replied that the great Chief of the Ottawas might enter but the crowd he had with him must remain outside.

Pontiac told the major that he wanted all his warriors to enjoy the fragrance of the friendly calumet, and if all could not enter, none would do so.

Gladwyn answered bluntly that he would have none of Pontiac's rabble in his fort.

This insulting repulse tore aside the mask of friendliness that had been maintained between the two leaders in the past.

Pontiac turned toward his warriors, speechless with rage and lifted his brawny arm in a gesture of defiance to signal that the moment they were waiting for had come.

Howling their war cries, they leaped to their feet and scattered to search for English blood to spill and English scalps to lift.

Major Henry Gladwyn

9

THE SIEGE OF
FORT DETROIT BEGINS

PONTIAC TOOK NO PART in the bloody forays of his warriors. He pushed a canoe from the bank and paddled furiously toward his village on the other shore. Yelling at the women and children and old men who had been left behind, he ordered them to prepare for moving the camp to the western shore, on the same side as the fort so he and his men would be closer to the fort.

Instantly the squaws began the task of moving.

Weapons, utensils, provisions, even the bark slabs that covered the lodges were carried to the bank ready to be loaded into the canoes.

At nightfall the warriors returned from their marauding.

Pontiac waited for them to assemble; then he appeared in his usual dramatic fashion, painted and feathered and brandishing a tomahawk.

As the fires were lighted and the drums sounded their rhythmic thumping, he began his war dance — stamping on the ground, leaping high and stabbing at the air with fierce gestures while he yelled for vengeance against the invaders of the Indians' land.

In seconds the warriors were caught up in the spirit of the dance and crowded about their leader, wheeling and circling, and howling defiance of the English.

After the war dance ended, the move to the other shore was started. Before daylight the whole Ottawa band had crossed the river and pitched their wigwams on the western side, just above the mouth of a small stream called Parents Creek.

Next morning the war spirit still burned brightly in Pontiac's heart. He gathered his own men and his Wyandot, Potawatomie and Chippewa allies and led them in a fierce attack on the fort.

The Indians, hiding behind barns and fences, among bushes and trees or lying flat in hollows on the ground, poured their fire at the palisades. Some who could not find places of shelter tried to dodge the fire from the fort by leaping and running. They filled their mouths with bullets and loaded and fired without stopping their gyrations.

The garrison fired from the loopholes in the fort's bastions; the fur traders inside answered the Indian howls with their own equally ferocious yells. Some of the Ottawas were able to get close to the walls. They holed up in a house owned by the interpreter, La Butte, and fired on the fort and at the vessel anchored off the corner of the fort, doing little damage.

The exchange of fire went on for six grueling hours with nothing accomplished. At last the Indians grew tired of the affair and slackened their fire. Their yells died away.

Pontiac, seeing no profit in exhausting his men and ammunition, called them off with a mighty thrust of his arm and they withdrew from the fort area.

The chief sent messengers to warn the French habitants they must not take provisions into the fort nor aid the garrison in any way, or they would be killed. The habitants had previously brought green vegetables and other supplies to sell to the English soldiers.

Gladwyn thought the attack was merely a sudden outburst of hostility that would fade away in a short time. However, since he needed provisions for his garrison in case it turned out to be a real war, he decided to send his interpreter, La Butte, to Pontiac's camp for a parley with the chief. La Butte was to find out the reason for the attack on the fort and assure Pontiac that Major Gladwyn was willing to adjust any real grievance.

Accompanied by two elderly Canadians, La Butte set out for Pontiac's village.

At the camp, Pontiac met the three ambassadors with seeming friendliness and appeared to agree to their proposal for peace.

La Butte hurried back to the fort to report that his mission had been successful. He said he thought a few gifts to the Indians would settle the matter. However, when he went to the camp a second time, he found that no decision had been made — Pontiac had evaded every effort to persuade him into giving a firm yes or no.

Immediately on La Butte's return, Pontiac called the chiefs into a consultation among themselves. They came back shortly and Pontiac as spokesman declared that they desired a lasting peace but wanted to hold council with their English fathers themselves. He asked that Captain Campbell come to the camp.

Major Gladwyn was reluctant to let his second officer go to Pontiac's camp but Captain Campbell said he had no fear of the Indians as he had always been on friendly terms with them.

Lieutenant McDugall volunteered to go along with him and they left the fort accompanied by La Butte and several Canadians.

As the little party crossed the wooden bridge over Parents Creek and approached Pontiac's camp, they saw a large gathering of Indians coming to meet them. The women caught up sticks and clubs and ran toward the red-coated officers as if they would make them run the gauntlet, a fate reserved for prisoners of war. It usually meant a cruel and lingering death to the victim.

At that moment Pontiac stepped into the crowd. He quieted the Indians, led the visitors through the camp to his lodge, and seated them on mats placed on the ground. The chief spoke a few words, to which Captain Campbell replied, and then the entire population of the camp crowded into the lodge to gaze at the white officers. They filed in and out for an hour until the captain, who now realized his dangerous position, rose and said he was going to return to the fort.

Pontiac signalled him to resume his seat, saying:

"My father will sleep tonight in the lodge of his red children."

Some of the Indians suggested killing the English captives on the spot but Pontiac protected them from injury and led them to quarters in the Meloche house, near Parents Creek, where they were placed under guard.

A crestfallen La Butte returned to the fort that evening to give the commander Pontiac's terms for peace and the disturbing news about the two officers being detained. The peace terms were the same terms the English had exacted from the French at the surrender of the fort — they must lay down their arms, give up their baggage (stores) and leave under Indian escort.

Major Gladwyn's florid face turned purple and his eyes flashed blue fire when he learned that the two British officers had been held in the Indian camp. It was against Indian tradition to harm an emissary. The commander used strong and violent language in replying that he refused to consider the matter until his two officers were returned unharmed. He said he had not been sent to Detroit to surrender the fort and suggested Pontiac save his ammunition for hunting.

Pontiac, proud of his coup in outsmarting the major, sent

word of his catch to his allies, the Potawatomies and the Hurons.

The next morning after the detention of the British officers, Pontiac and several of his chiefs crossed the river to the Wyandot village to recruit the Christianized Hurons in his crusade. This small band under their chief, Teata, had remained neutral because of their priest, but under pressure from the chief, they agreed to take part in the siege after mass on Holy Thursday (Ascension Day). Pontiac said they could come in later.

He set up ambushes along the river bank, below the fort and in the woods to entrap any Englishmen who tried to reach the fort by land or water.

On May 11, after firing at the fort for most of the day, Pontiac sent a Canadian with a message to Major Gladwyn. The Ottawa chief demanded the surrender of the fort and promised that the English would be allowed to go on their vessels unmolested, leaving their arms and other possessions behind.

Gladwyn, with characteristic British bulldog stubbornness, again refused to consider giving up his fort.

Unknown to Pontiac, the officers of the garrison held an emergency session to decide what could be done. Most of the men were in favor of embarking in the vessels and sailing to Niagara. They were short of food, having only a three-weeks supply of salt pork. There was little chance that a supply of provisions could reach them before that ran out.

There was also a constant threat of burning arrows being shot into the fort and setting fire to the wooden houses with their straw thatched roofs.

Still another worry was that the Indians would unite in a general onslaught and batter or burn an entrance through the wooden pickets of the palisade. However, a Canadian living in the fort, who knew the Indians well, assured the English soldiers that Pontiac would not risk the life of a single warrior by assaulting the fort in hand-to-hand fashion. It was not the Indian way of war.

Under the watchful eyes of the guards, soldiers from the garrison burned outbuildings, fences and orchard trees surrounding the fort so the Indians would have no shelter from which to fire.

The two vessels in the river patrolled the northern and southern ends of the fort to keep them clear.

Tiny St. Anne's church, inside the walls of the fort, was not a target. The priest of the settlement threatened Pontiac with vengeance of the Great Spirit if it were harmed and the chief ordered it preserved.

At night a few Canadians, who lived on the opposite side of the river, brought cattle, hogs and other provisions in boats to help supply the hungry garrison. The Indians failed to detect them for some time.

Pontiac, while directing the course of the siege, was continuing his efforts to get the commander to surrender. The chief assured Gladwyn by messenger that if he gave up the fort, he and his garrison could leave on the vessels, but if he defended it to the last man as he had said he would, the Englishmen would be treated as Indians treat other Indians captured in war — they would be burned alive.

Gladwyn sent back an answer saying he cared nothing for threats. He would do as he had said — defend his fort to the last man.

Encouraged by Gladwyn's stout resistance, the garrison carried on, sleeping in their clothes while on watch and keeping their guns at the ready. Inside the walls, tubs of water were placed at intervals to douse fires started by flaming arrows, and the garrison set a day and night guard over the fort's palisade walls.

10

CUYLER'S EXPEDITION

WHEN PONTIAC received a reinforcement of one hundred and twenty Chippewas from Grand River, it gave him fresh enthusiasm and he directed a new attack on the fort. However, the firing did little damage and the chief called off the attack to wait until the Master-of-Life favored him.

After two weeks of siege, Pontiac and his allies were beginning to tighten their belts. The warriors were hungry and the children cried for food.

The chief had not thought to lay in a stock of provisions. He believed that the siege would last only a few days, then he would have access to the stores in the fort.

At night the daring young braves raided the fields and stock pens of the habitants. Some of the older Frenchmen decided to do something about it. Fifteen of them called on Pontiac to complain about the raids.

When Pontiac saw them approaching his camp, he thought they were coming to offer aid for his project and advanced to meet them. Instead of waiting for the Canadians to state their errand as was Indian protocol, Pontiac eagerly inquired why they had come.

At this, the white-haired leader of the delegation faced the chief with angry eyes and boldly stated his errand.

"You pretend," he said, "to be friends of the French and yet you plunder us of our hogs and cattle, you trample upon our fields of young corn and, when you enter our houses, you enter with tomahawk raised. When your French father comes from Montreal with his great army, he will hear of what you have done and, instead of shaking hands with you as brethren, he will punish you as enemies."

Pontiac, head bowed, listened in silence.

When the old man had finished, the chief gave this answer: "Brothers: We have never wished to do you harm nor allow any to be done you; but among us there are many young men who, though strictly watched, will find opportunities of mischief." After neatly shifting the blame onto the irresponsible young men, Pontiac went on to declare:

> "It is not to revenge myself alone that I make war on the English. It is to revenge you, my brothers, when the English insulted us, they insulted you also. I know that they have taken away your arms, and made you sign a paper which they have sent to their country. Therefore you are left defenceless, and I mean now to revenge your cause and my own together. I mean to destroy the English and leave not one upon our lands. You do not know the reason from which I act. I have told you those only which concern yourselves, but you will learn all in time. You will cease then to think me a fool. I know, my brothers, that there are many among you who take part with the English. I am sorry for it for their own sakes, for when our father arrives (king of France) I shall point them out to him and they will see whether they or I have most reason to be satisfied with the part we have played.
>
> "I do not doubt, my brothers, that this war is very troublesome to you, for our warriors are continually passing and repassing through your settlement. I am sorry for it. Do not think that I approve of the damage that is done by them and, as proof of this, remember the war with the Foxes and the part I took in it."

Pontiac ran his eyes over the French delegation and a stern look on his face reflected the grim memory of past battles in support of the French. He continued.

"It is now seventeen years since the Chippewas of Michilimackinac combined with the Sacs and the Foxes, came down to destroy you. Who then defended you? Was it not I and my young men? Machinac, great chief of all these nations, said in council that he would carry to his village the head of your commandant — that he would eat his heart and drink his blood. Did I not take your part? Did I not go to his camp and say to him that if he wished to kill the French, he must first kill me and my warriors? Did I not assist you in routing them and driving them away? And now you think that I would turn my arms against you? No, my brothers, I am the same French Pontiac who assisted you seventeen years ago. I am á Frenchman and I wish to die a Frenchman; and now I repeat to you that you and I are one — that it is for both our interests that I should be revenged. Let me alone! I do not ask for your aid, for it is not in your power to give it. I only ask for provisions for myself and men. Yet, if you are inclined to assist me, I shall not refuse you. It would please me and you yourselves would be sooner rid of your troubles; for I promise you that, as soon as the English are driven out, we will go back to our villages and there await the arrival of our French father."

Pontiac paused to let this promise have an effect before finishing his speech.

"You have heard what I have to say. Remain at peace, and I will watch that no harm shall be done to you, either by my men or by the other Indians."

With these final words Pontiac shook hands with the French delegation and dissolved the council.

Immediately he began to carry out his promises by forbidding the warriors to raid the Frenchmen's farms and stock pens. He visited the families and assigned to each one a certain amount of provisions that it should furnish the Indians. All supplies were to be taken to the home of Monsieur Meloche, near Parents Creek in the fort area.

Pontiac put an elderly French resident in charge of this commissary to insure that only the urgent needs of the Indians would be met.

In return the chief, although without property of any kind, issued promissory notes (probably the first ever drawn for such purposes) etched on pieces of birchbark and signed with the figure of an otter, Pontiac's totem. It is reported that all these notes were redeemed by payment in furs.

As the days grew warmer and the ice left the lakes, Pontiac kept a watchful eye on the fort and ordered his warriors to patrol the river in their canoes.

The chief learned that General Amherst had sent a detachment of troops under Lieutenant Cuyler up the lakes to deliver supplies and ammunition to the fort and that Major Gladwyn and his garrison were anxiously awaiting the arrival of the convoy of boats. The besieged Englishmen were now on scant rations of a pound of bread and two ounces of salt pork per man per day.

The commander thought to hurry the reinforcements by ordering the *Michigan*, one of his two vessels that guarded the fort, to sail to Niagara and meet the convoy.

Pontiac held the fort under constant guard to see that no Englishman showed his head above the palisades. He sent messengers to the Illinois country to ask his old friend, Major Neyon de Villiers, who commanded there, to send troops to help him fight the English.

When the chief learned that the *Michigan* had set sail to meet the convoy but was becalmed at the entrance of Lake Erie, he set up a scheme to capture it.

While the *Michigan* waited for a favorable wind, a fleet of canoes darted from the shore and surrounded her. In the prow of the first canoe Captain Campbell was held captive in the hope that the master of the vessel would hold his fire rather than risk the life of the British officer.

However, Captain Campbell boldly yelled at the crew to follow their orders without regard to him. Luckily for the British, at that instant a fresh breeze sprang up, the sails filled and the sloop set out toward Niagara.

Pontiac refused to punish Captain Campbell for his action, but he was taken back to Meloche's house still a prisoner of Pontiac.

On May 30 the garrison was aroused by the news that the convoy was in sight in the river.

There was loud rejoicing as the soldiers, traders and habitants hurried to the water gate to cheer the arrival of food and men. They could see the line of boats with the British ensign flying from the stern of the foremost one. The bastion defied the enemy and welcomed their friends with a cannon shot.

Then, to the horror of the watchers, naked figures stood up in the boats and a war whoop sounded over the water.

The garrison stood in horrified silence as they realized that the convoy had fallen into the hands of the Indians and the troops were their captives.

In each of the eighteen boats, two or more disarmed soldiers were forced to row while Indians guarded them. Along the shore a line of natives followed on foot to make sure no English prisoners escaped.

Unexpectedly, the steersman in the foremost boat, which contained four soldiers and only three Indians, turned aside toward the vessel guarding the approach to the fort and began yelling for help.

One of the British soldiers seized the principal Indian by the hair, gripped his belt with the other hand, lifted him and plunged him into the river. While the boat rocked with their struggles, the Indian held fast to the Englishman's clothing and trailed along in the water. Then he lifted himself up, stabbed the soldier with his knife and dragged the body overboard into the swift current where both men drowned still locked in combat.

The other two Indians leaped from the boat. The soldiers pulled for the vessel and yelled for help.

Canoes came paddling swiftly after them and the natives on shore fired at them. The birch canoes were gaining on the getaway boat but just when escape seemed impossible, the vessel fired at the pursuing canoes and set them back.

Another ball from the vessel's cannon scattered the Indians on shore and allowed the men in the boat to reach the vessel with the supplies they had on board.

The vessel then moved on to the fort and reported the loss of the other boats and men.

That night several Canadians came to the fort and told the garrison the fate of the other Englishmen in the convoy.

They said the Indians, fearing that the barges might escape as the foremost one had done, landed the remaining prisoners, tied them and conducted them to the Ottawa village and on to Pontiac's camp. As soon as all the warriors had gathered, they herded their captives onto the beach, made them strip themselves and shot arrows into their bodies.

Some of the prisoners tried to throw themselves on the ground to avoid the arrows but they were beaten with sticks and forced to stand up until they fell dead; after which those Indians who had not fired fell upon their bodies, cut them into pieces, and reportedly cooked and ate them. Other captives they tormented by cutting their flesh with flints or piercing them with lances. They then cut off their hands and feet and left them weltering in their blood.

Some of the unfortunate prisoners were fastened to stakes and burned. No kind of torture was left untried. It was the customary victory celebration and even the women joined in the bloody excesses of the drunken warriors.

A few men among the English prisoners were chosen for adoption. They were to serve as slaves for the Indians who claimed them — a life hardly more desirable than death. However, a few of the slaves managed to escape later or were purchased by traders and released.

When the orgy was over, many of the bodies were left on shore. The remainder were thrown into the river where they floated downstream past the fort within sight of their former comrades.

The Wyandots, important allies of Pontiac, were credited with this valuable capture of supplies consisting of provisions, ammunition and rum. The rum may have been responsible for the revenge inflicted on the captured men, although torture and death were commonplace events in Indian warfare. It had always been so and was the accepted treatment.

Later Lieutenant Cuyler told his story of the incident. He had landed at Point Pelee, not far from the mouth of the Detroit River, on the 28th day of May. He ordered the boats drawn up on the beach and camped there for the night.

Before dawn while the English troops were still sleeping, an old man gathering firewood gave the alarm — "Indians!" — and the troops stumbled into formation before the boats.

Suddenly a volley of fire came from the woods. The Indians broke into the open and rushed the line of British soldiers. The troops threw down their guns in panic and ran to the boats. They tried to shove them into the water and managed to get five boats afloat.

The terrified soldiers, trying to get away from Indians' fire, crowded into the five boats and shoved off from shore. Lieutenant Cuyler was able to get into one of them. The Indians followed swiftly after them and caught three of the boats. The thirty-two soldiers in the two remaining boats rowed all night and landed in the morning upon a small island.

Cuyler set out for Fort Sandusky but on arrival there

found the fort burned to the ground. He then went along the south shore to Presque Isle and on back to Niagara to report to General Amherst.

A few weeks after the ambush word was brought to Pontiac's camp that the officer (Lieutenant Cuyler) and thirty-two men who escaped from the ambush of the convoy were in the Sandusky Islands. Pontiac ordered them tracked down and caught before they could carry the word of the ambush to Niagara. He sent fifty men to notify the three hundred who were scouting the lake that they should combine forces and capture them.

However, Lieutenant Cuyler and his men and the two barges were by then well on their way to Niagara.

Lieutenant Cuyler filed this report of his escape:

"Being abandoned by my men, I was forced to retreat in the best manner I could. I was left with six men on the beach, endeavoring to get off a boat, which not being able to effect, was obliged to run up to my neck in the lake to get to a boat that had pushed off without my knowledge. When I was in the lake, I saw five boats manned, and the Indians having manned two boats, pursued and brought back three of the five, keeping a continued fire from off the shore, and from the two boats that followed us, about a mile on the lake. The wind springing up fair, I and the other remaining boat hoisted sail and escaped."

11

INDIANS TAKE OVER
THE BRITISH FORTS

TRUE TO THEIR WORD — or in fear of reprisals from the Ottawa chief — on Thursday after mass, Teata's Hurons united with the Potawatomies who were posted below the fort. Their war whoops gave Pontiac the signal to start firing from above the fort and the two forces kept up a heavy barrage throughout the day.

One party of Indians dashed from the woods and found cover in barns behind the fort, but they were routed when Major Gladwyn set the barns on fire with hot shot from his three-pounder. In this affray the natives lost several warriors.

That evening Pontiac sent a message to Gladwyn asking for another truce for the burial of the dead. This request was granted. He still kept his prisoners, Campbell and McDugall, captive in Meloche's house.

The months of May and June, 1763, saw the lonely forts scattered among the lakes (all of which had been occupied by the British after the French surrender) fall into the hands of the Indians. Some of the garrisons were wiped out entirely while others lost their commanders and many of their men. Most of the captives, if they survived the celebration of the

victory, were brought to Pontiac's camp to be shown to the
chief. They were then claimed by their captors. By tribal law
the Indian who first seized an Englishman by the hair owned
him and could do as he wished with the unfortunate prisoner.

After the capture of white prisoners, particularly British
troops, almost the first act was to strip them of their clothing.
The Indians considered the brilliant red coats, the gold braid
and the other decorations symbols of white superiority and
wanted to divest their prisoners of any object that set them
apart. Also it helped to prevent their escape.

To the south on the lower Detroit River, Pontiac had set
up an ambush of "bad", meaning unchristianized, Hurons,
watching for reinforcements of soldiers or traders going to the
fort. They caught two traders and captured a five-boat cargo
from Niagara consisting of rum, trade goods and seventeen
barrels of gunpowder.

This was reported to the fort on Friday morning, May 13,
by a Frenchman who gave the additional information that the
Hurons had taken on so much of the captured rum that they
were helplessly drunk.

Gladwyn sent twenty-five men under Captain Hopkins
to take the sloop down river, burn the Huron village and bring
back the powder. But the wind turned against them and they
were signalled to return. It was learned later that the Hurons
were not only sober but waiting to ambush the sloop. Some of
the French carried false information in order to trick the
British or to harass them.

At this time Pontiac's men brought news of the taking of
Fort Sandusky by the Wyandot band from that area, aided by
the Detroit band. Only a few men of the British garrison survived, and the fort was set on fire.

The fort commander, Ensign Paully (Pauli) was brought
bound hand and foot to Pontiac's camp.

A crowd of Indians, mostly women and children, met

him with sticks and stones and proceeded to pelt him with them. He was unbound and forced to dance and sing for their amusement while being reminded that death at the stake awaited him.

Fortunately Ensign Paully was spared this cruel fate. An old squaw, lately widowed, offered to take the personable young commander as her husband and he agreed to this rather than face the torture of death by fire.

First he was taken to the river and plunged into the water to wash the white blood from his veins, then led to the lodge of his bride, after which he was treated as an Ottawa warrior.

This capture of Sandusky had been planned by Pontiac — and he spoke of it as his own coup because the same method he had used in his attempt to take Fort Detroit was successful in taking Fort Sandusky. A few Indians (Hurons) had asked for a council, then suddenly produced weapons and cut down the garrison in a savage surprise move. They took the commander prisoner and burned the fort.

Pontiac's strategy in setting up this action was the first step in his campaign against the forts outside Detroit.

Fort St. Joseph (Niles, Michigan), Fort Miamis (Fort Wayne, Indiana), Fort Ouatanon (Lafayette, Indiana) and three Pennsylvania forts, Venango (Franklin), Le Boeuf (Waterford) and Presque Isle (Erie), were taken. Their commanders were killed or captured. The garrisons were murdered or taken prisoner and the forts plundered. Fort Venango was burned to the ground. Fort Edward Augustus (Green Bay, Wisconsin) was abandoned in the middle of June.

Pontiac felt a tremendous sense of power as each capture was reported to him and the loot divided. He regarded each conquest as a personal triumph, and a sign that the Master-of-Life was favoring his cause.

The Ottawa chief had devised a scheme for taking the important Fort Michilimackinac at the top of Lake Michigan

in the area where he was born. He knew that the capture of
this fort, larger than most of the others and garrisoned with
thirty-five men under command of Captain George Etherington, would be difficult and dangerous.

Pontiac planned to be present in person and direct the
attack but early in June a band of Chippewas, not in Pontiac's
confederation, got ahead of the chief by means of a game.

Lacrosse (Baug-ah-ud-o-way, pronounced *Baggittaway*)
was the Indians' favorite sport. They invented it and played it
with enthusiasm, strength and great skill. This popular sport
required two goal posts, a ball made of deerskin stuffed with
hair, and a long-handled racket called a *crosse*. The object of
the game was to catch the ball in the racket, run with it, and
hurl it through the goal posts of the opposing team. Usually
there were twelve players on each team, but sometimes a village would challenge a neighboring village and the entire
population of men and boys would appear in the lineup.

Lacrosse was a rough game and often caused serious injury to those engaged. A player who was hurt was expected to
drop out of the action and hide from the eyes of his friends
and the spirits that watched over the games. He had shamed
them by playing poorly.

On the king's birthday, June 4, the men in the garrison of
Fort Michilimackinac were relaxing from their usual discipline.
The sun was warm and the air refreshing, there were no eagle
feathers in sight, and no Indian howls spoiled the peaceful
atmosphere.

Late in the morning, an apparently friendly band of Chippewas wandered into the area and invited the soldiers to watch
their game of lacrosse. The sports-loving English accepted and
posted themselves outside the stockade to see the contest.

It was an exciting and noisy game the Indians put on for
the soldiers. Hordes of women and children crowded the side-
lines and cheered for the players.

Suddenly, in a moment of lively play, the ball was accidentally — or by intent — thrown over the palisades wall into the fort.

Immediately the players forgot about the game and rushed inside, followed by the women. The men grasped weapons that the squaws had concealed in their clothing and before the soldiers could arm themselves, the Indians were upon them. The Chippewas clubbed and slashed at the Englishmen in a vicious attack, cutting off their heads and limbs, and in a few wild-swinging minutes twenty of the garrison's force were massacred. The Indians made prisoners of the soldiers left alive and then looted the stock of trade goods in the fort, obtaining a large amount of powder and lead.

Pontiac learned of the fall of Fort Michilimackinac with mixed emotions — keen resentment and jealousy because he was not consulted before the attack took place and a feeling of happiness that his crusade against the English was going well.

Late in the month of June, the Delawares sent word to the commander at Fort Pitt advising him that the other forts had fallen and suggesting he had better give up Fort Pitt before an army of Indians descended upon it.

Swiss Captain Ecuyler, the commander, replied that he could defend his fort with his force of over three hundred men. He urged the chiefs to make peace.

Smallpox was in his camp and he gave the Delawares blankets from the smallpox hospital. He may have considered exposing the Indians to this malady (fatal at that time) as legal as shooting them and perhaps more effective. It was reported that smallpox raged among the Shawnees and Mingoes through the summer and into the following year.

While the other forts were being taken according to his planned strategy, Pontiac was still trying to come up with the answer to his own immediate problem of taking Fort Detroit.

Indians Playing Lacrosse

He felt a great surge of pride and confidence in his power when the bands came to him bringing prisoners and loot from the captured forts and told of their success in using the strategy he had taught them. However, the sound of the sunset gun that fired each evening to let the vessels know the fort was still in English hands and the sight of the British flag still flying over Fort Detroit were constant reminders of his failure to take his own objective. He burned with desire to oust the English from it and have revenge on them.

Often at sunrise Pontiac stood on the shore of Lake Erie watching the first rays of light gild the rippling waters with color. He lifted brawny arms toward the east and petitioned the Master-of-Life to give his medicine power over the English and let the red children live in the land He had created for them.

12

MAJOR GLADWYN
DEFIES BESIEGERS

As THE SIEGE CONTINUED Pontiac was joined by Wasson, a chief of the Chippewas, who brought two hundred warriors to the Ottawa camp. A council was held and the resulting decision was to cease firing at Fort Detroit and make war on all persons seeking to assist the garrison with reinforcements or supplies. Immediately the Ottawas, Potawatomies, Hurons and Chippewas left on a mission to scout the lake and capture any Englishmen or any English sympathizers they could find.

On the night of June 2, one of the prisoners of the Ottawas, an English soldier, escaped naked from the camp and gained the fort. He was bearing a letter for Major Gladwyn that Captain Campbell had given him before helping him to get away. The letter had been taken by the Hurons from the captured convoy and brought to Pontiac, and he had given it to Campbell to read. It was written by an officer at Niagara to the commander at Fort Miamis and told of the treaty of peace having been signed between the British and the French.

The fort put on a band concert that evening to celebrate the signing of the treaty. On the following day Gladwyn sum-

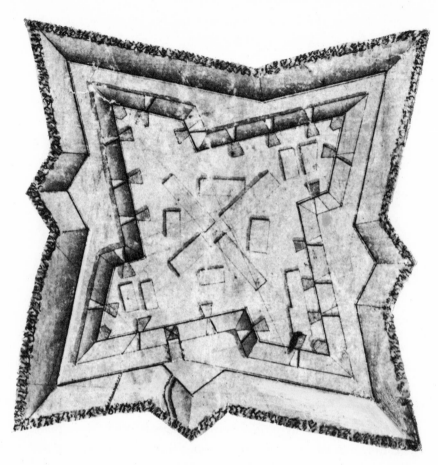

A Plan of Fort Detroit, 1760

moned all the French living in the fort and had the letter read
to them, letting them know that the peace treaty between
England and France had been finally concluded and that, by
agreement between the two, Canada and all the Illinois country was now English territory.

Pontiac had asked La Butte to translate the letter that was
later taken to Gladwyn. The chief stood with shoulders
squared and eyes narrowed as against an ill wind while the
disturbing news was read to him. Then he said he could not
understand how two kings an ocean away could make a treaty

transferring the Indians' land that neither of them owned or had ever seen. It was hard for him to believe that the French, friends and allies of the tribes for generations, had switched to the side of an old enemy.

The chief told his warriors that their great father, the king of France, had fallen asleep, but he would awaken and come to the aid of his red children and they must fight the English and watch for their French father and his soldiers.

On June 11 Pontiac's warriors saw a band of twenty men from the garrison burn the last building, a house and a shop, which had sheltered the Indians while they made forays against the fort. They also saw the soldiers work over the barges and boats beached in front. They knew the English were making preparations in case they should be starved out and have to abandon the fort. They could use these craft and the sloop to get to Niagara.

Pontiac's camp was quiet for a few days. The braves kept to their lodges while the rain-bringing spirits rolled thunder, flashed lightning, and the skies opened.

When Pontiac's spies informed him that a trader had brought two canoe-loads of goods and liquor and the Potawatomies had already exacted two barrels of wine, the chief was determined to get his share. He crossed the river and ordered the trader to move his goods to a Frenchman's house which was near Pontiac's camp. "For your own safety," the chief suavely told the trader, and the trader gave up five barrels of liquor for the guarantee of protection.

On June 19th the vessel that Gladwyn had sent down Lake Erie to hasten the convoy was returning from Niagara.

The *Michigan* had missed Cuyler's troops on her way but proceeded to Niagara and waited there until Cuyler with the two boats and the men who had escaped the ambush at Point Pelee returned to Niagara. Then Lieutenant Cuyler and his men and a small detachment of troops from the garrison there

were ordered to return to Detroit in the sloop. They had
drawn within sight of the fort when the wind failed and the
vessel dropped down to wait for a better opportunity to come
up to the fort.

In the meantime Pontiac's scouts had reported it in sight
below the fort and the chief alerted his forces to attack it from
Turkey Island where they had erected a breastwork of logs.
Soon several hundred Indians were waiting in ambush for the
vessel to move on.

Major Gladwyn ordered two cannon shots to let the
troops on board know that the fort was still holding out. After
waiting several days the sloop made a second attempt to sail up
to the fort. The river channel was narrow in places and the
danger point was yet to be passed.

The Indians hiding on the island could see only a few
men on deck and resolved to make their attack that night. At
the blackest hour they muffled their paddles and slipped quietly
into the water.

However, the watchman on the vessel saw dark shapes
moving toward them and summoned others of the crew who
were hiding below. These men silently took their posts on the
deck. They agreed the blow of a hammer on the mast was to
be the signal to fire. When the canoes were within a few rods,
the vessel suddenly erupted in a burst of cannon and musket
fire, illuminating the scene like a flash of lightning. The shots
tore into the canoes, destroyed several of them, and killed and
wounded a number of Indians.

Pontiac's men found that instead of the half dozen Englishmen they thought were on board, the vessel had a full
crew of sixty or more. They pulled away and paddled to shore
where they fired at the sloop from behind their breastwork
of logs.

The next week on Monday, Pontiac renewed his war. He
dictated a letter to be delivered to Gladwyn and forced Captain

Campbell to write it. In the letter Pontiac told the commander that he and his men must leave the fort at once because the great Chippewa chief, Minavavana, and his son Kinonchamek, were on their way to the Ottawa camp with eight hundred warriors. He said they would aid in the capture of the fort and that he himself would not be able to control the wild Chippewas after they had overcome the garrison. He warned there was great danger to all within the fort and urged the commander to surrender at once.

Major Gladwyn's vehement reply was the same as he had given before — that until his officers, Captain Campbell and Lieutenant McDugall were returned unharmed, there would be no discussion between him and the chief.

This resistance so infuriated Pontiac that he sent back a threatening letter saying he kept the two officers (Campbell and McDugall) to prevent their being boiled with the rest of the garrison. He said that the fire under the kettle had already been lighted.

After this exchange of thought, the fort signalled the sloop with cannon shots and the band played in the bastion facing her. Two days later the wind came up and the vessel lifted anchor and made it to her berth in front of the fort. Pontiac was hardly able to control his rage when he learned of its safe arrival.

On board were Lieutenant Cuyler and the thirty-two men who had escaped from the captured convoy. The lieutenant brought letters to Major Gladwyn confirming news of the peace treaty having been signed in Paris by both the English and the French monarchs.

By this treaty the French residents of the area became British subjects instead of neutrals merely watching the English and the Indians battle each other.

Many of the Canadians began to spread the word that the news of the peace treaty signing was only a story invented by

Gladwyn to keep the Indians quiet. They assured Pontiac that their father, the king of France, would never abandon his red children, and that a great French army was even then coming to their aid by way of the St. Lawrence River while another was approaching by way of the Illinois River. This was something Pontiac wanted to believe and he proclaimed it to his warriors with eloquent words and gestures.

Early the following morning it was discovered that Lieutenant McDougall and three other English prisoners had escaped and reached the fort. They reported that Captain Campbell had declined to break away with them, saying he was nearsighted and too fat to take the chance.

For the next few days no Indians ventured within gunshot of the fort. Not one eagle feather was silhouetted against the sky.

Occasionally there were two cannon shots from the fort, a pre-arranged signal to the vessels anchored in the lake near the mouth of the river that the fort was still in English hands and they could come up to it.

Pontiac's camp had visitors — Father Jonois (Du Jaunay) a Jesuit priest and a missionary to the Ottawas, came from Michilimackinac accompanied by seven Ottawas and eight Chippewas.

Father Jonois lodged with the Huron missionary. The next morning he went to the fort with a letter from Captain Etherington, whose fort at Michilimackinac had been overrun. Captain Etherington asked for help — troops, ammunition and supplies — but Major Gladwyn replied that he was being assaulted by Pontiac and could do nothing. Father Jonois then set out on the long canoe journey back to his far north post.

Pontiac's Indian visitors were under the command of Kinonchamek, son of Minavavana, called "Le Grand Sauteur" (The Great Chippewa), an important chief and an ally of Pontiac.

They camped two miles above the fort, and the Indians came to welcome them in the name of their own chiefs. Kinonchamek said he and his men had come to see Pontiac and counsel with him.

Pontiac then ordered the warriors of each of the nations in the Detroit area to stay in their camps for the day and listen to the speech of the great chief of the Chippewas, Minavavana, brought to them by his son, Kinonchamek.

Before the council began, two canoe-loads of Shawnees and Delawares from the Ohio River area arrived. On hearing that Kinonchamek was there, the Shawnees and Delawares went to his camp to learn the purpose of the visit.

Early in the afternoon Kinonchamek and his men joined the new arrivals and all went to Pontiac's camp to attend the council that Pontiac had called to honor the son of Minavavana. The assembled chiefs seated themselves in a circle and waited in silence for the conference to begin.

13

PONTIAC
HOLDS COUNCIL

THE VISITING CHIEF spoke first. He chided Pontiac for the bad behavior of his warriors. He referred to the massacre of the garrisons of captured forts as "glutting themselves with blood."

While Pontiac stood silent, Kinonchamek said that his warriors had killed only in battle and that their captives were sent to Montreal alive and unharmed. He also stressed the fact that *his* people had not harmed the French residents while Pontiac, in contrast, had put pressure on the French to join him against the English. Besides that, the Ottawas' constant theft of French provisions and livestock was shameful.

The son of Minavavana faced Pontiac and directly accused him of killing white prisoners, of drinking their blood and eating their flesh. This, he said, was not good. The Master-of-Life had placed deer and other game in the forest for his children to eat. Kinonchamek pointed out that his own people had laid in provisions to feed themselves and their families, and that if Pontiac had done this, he would not now be in such dire need of supplies or in danger of incurring the wrath of their great father (king of France) by robbing the French inhabitants.

Pontiac stood without change of expression during this cutting speech, reluctant to say that his warriors had acted without his consent. The chief needed the Chippewas and their warriors to help carry out his grand plot against the English, and in spite of his own power and influence he dared not risk offending Minavavana. The confederation meant more to Pontiac than wounded pride.

After Kinonchamek had finished, the chief of the Erie band spoke for his people and the Delawares.

He rebuked Pontiac for harassing the French. He said that the Master-of-Life had told the Indians that killing in war was right, but after the fort had been taken, it was wrong to kill or to drink the blood of victims or eat the flesh of human beings. He referred to "his brothers" the French, who did not kill prisoners but exchanged them for French prisoners taken by the Indians.

Then slyly he ventured the assertion that the reason Pontiac did not restrain his warriors from cruel excesses in dealing with prisoners was that Pontiac had not been able to capture Fort Detroit and so took out his rage and resentment by allowing mistreatment of prisoners and harassment of the French habitants.

Finally, the Erie chief delivered a telling blow by asserting that he and his men had come with the intention of offering their assistance to Pontiac but now they would not. It was their fear that he would say it was the Erie chief and his band who had harmed the French. He added that he did not want to be blamed by the great father (king of France).

Most of the Indians still believed in the often-told story of the great army the French king would send to aid his red children in reclaiming their land from the English.

Pontiac, the eloquent voice of the Ottawas, for once had

no reply to offer his critics. He felt that the less he said the better. He could not deny the charges of bad conduct on the part of his warriors. He needed all the help he could get now and was trying desperately to retain his allies.

After the council was over, the visitors left for their own camps.

On July 2, Pontiac called his warriors to bring into his camp the older men and heads of families among the French habitants, intending to force them in joining his side of the war.

When all had asembled at the Ottawa camp and were seated on mats, Pontiac began his speech, addressing the French and handing them war belts as he spoke.

> "My brothers," he said, "how long will you suffer this bad flesh (the English) to remain upon your lands? I have told you before and I now tell you again, that when I took up the hatchet, it was for your good. This year the English must all perish throughout all Canada. The Master-of-Life commands it. And you, who know him better than we, wish to oppose his will. Until now I have said nothing on this matter. I have not urged you to take part with us in the war. It would have been enough had you been content to sit quiet on your mats, looking on, while we were fighting for you. But you have not done so. You call yourselves our friends, and yet you assist the English with provisions, and go about as spies among our villages. This must not continue. You must be wholly French or wholly English. If you are French, take up that war-belt and lift the hatchet with us, but if you are English, then we declare war upon you. My brothers, I know this is a hard thing. We are all alike children of our great father the king of France and it is hard to fight among brethren for the sake of dogs. But there is no choice. Look upon the belt, and let me have your answer."

One of the oldsters, holding a copy of the surrender of Canada and Detroit, rose to speak for the French.

He said their hands were tied by the command of the French king who had told them to remain quiet and regard the English as brothers until the time when the French should reclaim Canada. He reminded Pontiac that the chief had promised to wait for the return of the French, but now he was fighting the English and trying to force the French settlers into joining him.

Pontiac agreed to give the French oldsters time to consider his proposition. However, some of the irresponsible younger Frenchmen in the delegation picked up the war-belts, asserting that the young men would join Pontiac. They then boasted that it would be only a short while until the fort and all within would be captured.

At the close of the conference, the older men went to their homes but the younger ones who had declared themselves allies of Pontiac remained in the Indian camp. On the next day Pontiac's men held a celebration and a feast of roast dog for them. The chief assured them that when he had starved the Red Coats out of their fort, there would be rum for all.

One night after the feast, a party of the new recruits, joined by some Indians, went to the fort area and dug entrenchments from which to fire at the garrison. When daylight came, a detachment of soldiers ran from the fort and routed them. Two Indians were killed in the action.

One of the soldiers had been a prisoner of the Delawares and especially hated them. He knelt beside one of the dead Indian men, lifted his scalp and shook it at the fleeing Indians. This insulting gesture caused great resentment and anger among the tribesmen.

As an aftermath of Pontiac's council, one of the older Frenchmen who knew the chief well, returned the war-belt his son had accepted and told Pontiac how foolish it was to compel the French habitants to aid him against the British.

This man warned that when their father, the French king, returned, he would be displeased with his red children and
Pontiac would be blamed.

Pontiac said he and his Ottawas would not press the
French to join them. He accepted the returned war-belt.

When the unchristianized Huron band heard this, they
and the Potawatomies and the Chippewas threatened to force
the French to join *them* in fighting the English.

Major Gladwyn, on hearing of this supplied the habitants
with guns and ammunition and they began to stand guard and
keep watch against surprise attacks from the three Indian
nations.

On July 4, Ensign Pauli, former commander of the overrun fort at Sandusky, escaped and made a run for the fort.
When he was admitted he gave a report on the death of Captain Campbell.

The Indian who was shot and scalped by a soldier of the
garrison was a Chippewa chief, nephew of Wasson. Wasson
immediately blackened his face in mourning and went to
Pontiac, demanding that a captive of equal rank be turned over
to him.

Pontiac was reluctant to thus sign the death warrant of
one as courageous as Captain Campbell, but Wasson was an
ally and Indian justice was on his side. Pontiac could not refuse
to comply with this time-honored Indian custom.

Wasson took Captain Campbell to his own camp, stripped
him and tomahawked him. The captain's mutilated body was
thrown into the river and floated down stream where it was
recovered and buried with honors. Wasson had avenged his
nephew's death.

Pontiac still had a consuming desire to destroy the vessels
that guarded the fort. All his former efforts had failed but he
continued to fire upon them at intervals. Finally the chief and

his Chippewa allies hit upon a scheme to burn the sloop *Michigan* while it lay at anchor at the lower end of the fort.

Pontiac set his men to work building a raft that could be set afire, allowed to drift down river toward the big sloop and, hopefully, to set it aflame.

For the next several days everything was quiet at the fort while all hands at the Indian camp worked on the fire-raft — two boats tied together and filled with dry wood and bark. Before dawn on Sunday July 10, the raft was set on fire and turned loose to drift downriver. It was blazing fiercely but it passed within two hundred feet of the sloop and did no harm. The Indians had their work for nothing. Pontiac, raging with disappointment, ordered another raft built.

The plot to burn the sloop had been reported to Gladwyn.

At this time a band of Hurons, indifferent to Pontiac's threats or pleas, took seven prisoners to the fort and asked for peace terms. One of the prisoners was Lieutenant John Christie, who had been commander of the captured fort of Presque Isle.

Gladwyn demanded the return of the loot they had taken from the fort. They promised to bring it in.

On the next day, Monday, the Huron band took into the fort all the plundered trade goods they had and peace was declared between them and the English.

The second fire-raft Pontiac had ordered was ready. It was released that night but the sloop fired at it and broke it up before it could do any harm. Pontiac's medicine was not working for him. His nightly prayers grew lengthy and urgent as he appealed to the Master-of-Life for better luck.

For the next few days the Indians fired at the fort at intervals and the fort returned the fire, but little damage resulted on either side.

A new arrival at the fort was reported to Pontiac. He was André Huron of Loretto (near Quebec), a messenger between Fort Detroit and Fort Pitt.

On hearing of this, Pontiac and chiefs from the Ottawas

and Chippewas went to the Huron village to meet in council with the chiefs of the Eries and Delawares.

Three days later the messengers that Pontiac had sent to Major Neyon de Villiers, French commander of the Illinois country, returned with a discouraging report for their chief. They said that de Villiers had advised the Detroit Indians to remain on good terms with the French unless they were attacked. De Villiers also said he could offer Pontiac no aid because he had learned of the peace treaty being concluded and was expecting the British to send a garrison to take over his fort at any moment.

This alarming news called for a second council with the Eries, Delawares, Ottawas and Potawatomies. It also was held in the Huron village.

Pontiac, as head chief of all the nations, stood arrayed in the headdress and other colorful symbols of authority. After a stirring speech, he lifted a tomahawk and called upon the chiefs to join in his war-song, the theme of which was *drive the British from our land*.

The other chiefs fell in with his war-talk and after the council ended, they kept it up, whooping and yelling in their village throughout the night.

14

THE BATTLE OF
BLOODY RUN

On the 29th of July word was brought to Pontiac that before dawn, while a dense fog covered the river, an expedition of twenty-two barges had slipped between the Huron and the Potawatomie villages and reached the fort. The Indians fired upon them, killing and wounding several men.

The barges, under the command of Captain Dalyell, an aide-de-camp to General Amherst, carried two hundred soldiers, six cannon, and a large amount of provisions and ammunition. Also on board were Major Robert Rogers and twenty of his Rangers.

The barracks were too small to house the new arrivals and they were quartered upon the inhabitants.

Pontiac was greatly incensed because the convoy, a rich prize, had slipped past his guard in the fog.

The next morning the chief learned that all the troops had met on the parade ground and held an important conference and that Captain Dalyell had demanded permission to take a force of three hundred men and go to Pontiac's camp where they would make the Ottawa chief sue for peace. Major Gladwyn reluctantly granted it.

After receiving this information, Pontiac prepared a surprise for the impetuous Dalyell. He ordered all women and children hidden away from the camp, leaving only the old men. Then he posted two hundred and fifty of his warriors in an ambush on a farm only a half mile from the fort. Their orders were to lie low until the troops had passed, then block the retreat road.

Another band of one hundred and sixty warriors concealed themselves at a French house (Meloche's) where they had once camped and built strong entrenchments. In addition to this, sixty Indians were hidden behind a picket fence that faced the narrow wooden bridge over Parents Creek, where the troops would have to cross to reach the camp.

Pontiac's camp at that time was several miles above the mouth of Parents Creek and behind an extensive marsh that protected the lodges from the fire of the vessels as they patrolled the river.

The chief learned from his Canadian friends in the fort the exact time when the attack was planned and when the troops would leave the fort, then he made preparations. His warriors were ready for Captain Dalyell and his troops.

It was two o'clock on the morning of July 31st, 1763, when two hundred and fifty British soldiers filed noiselessly out the gates of the fort. They marched along the road in a double column with two bateaux, each having a swivel cannon on the bow, moving up the river abreast of them.

Lieutenant Brown led the advance force of twenty-five men; Captain Gray commanded the center and Captain Grant the rear.

The night was close and dark. Nothing stirred to warn the marching troops that Pontiac's warriors, with guns leveled upon them, could watch their every move from their hiding places behind the picket fences that enclosed the orchards and gardens of the French farm houses along the road.

Beyond the bridge on Parents Creek there were ridges running parallel to the river where Pontiac had made entrenchments while camped nearby.

Moving rapidly, the advance guard of English troops had reached the middle point of the bridge and the center section was just approaching it when a horrible din of whoops and yells arose. Indian guns blasted at them from in front and sides.

Half the men in the advance guard were shot down. Some of them fell into the creek below and stained the water with blood, giving the little stream a new name — *Bloody Run.*

The other men in the advance guard fell back in shock and dismay. The front ranks of the main section tried to retreat but their movements were blocked by others advancing onto the narrow structure.

In the confusion, Dalyell ran to the front and began to rally the men. He led them forward to the attack. The Indians poured in another volley and the troops again halted.

Dalyell shouted at them and they charged madly across the bridge and up the ridges beyond, but the enemy could not be seen. They continued to fire and their yells made the night hideous, but the English troops in the spooky darkness and in unfamiliar surroundings could not find them. It was decided to withdraw and wait for daylight rather than be cut to pieces by Indian fire.

Captain Grant recrossed the bridge with his company and stationed his men on the road. The remaining troops followed leaving a small party to place the dead and wounded on board the two bateaux which had rowed up to the bridge. Both sides kept up a sharp fire.

A large party of Indians gathered at Meloche's house but Captain Grant drove them from the house with bayonets. He found two Canadians inside who told him the Indians were gathering in the houses along the road below and planned to cut the English troops off from the fort. This news called for an immediate retreat. The command was given and the troops fell back into marching order and began moving back toward the fort with Captain Grant in the lead and Dalyell at the rear.

Some of the Indians followed the retreating troops and kept up a scattered fire. Occasionally the rear ranks of the British faced about and fired at their pursuers.

After half a mile the troops reached a place where the river ran close on their left and there were barns and out-buildings beyond stout picket fences on their right. Behind these pickets a great body of Indians waited to pounce upon them.

Pontiac's Ottawas and Chippewas formed the ambush at the bridge under his direct command. Later the Wyandots and the Potawatomies slipped through the woods behind the fort and joined in the battle.

The advance ranks passed unmolested but when the main body of the soldiers came opposite the ambush, the Indians raised the war whoop and poured a murderous fire into the ranks.

The soldiers, already unnerved by the unexpected calamities of the night, broke ranks and ran over each other trying to escape the hail of bullets. The retreat almost became a riot but Dalyell, already wounded, threatened and reprimanded his men, beating some of them with the flat of his sword until a sort of order was restored and the Indians' fire could be re-turned.

It was near dawn but a heavy mist still hung over the area. The troops could see only the flash of the Indians' guns and hear the terrifying war whoops.

The Indians holed up in a house by the side of the road and fired from the windows.

Major Rogers, with some of his Rangers, burst the door open with an axe and forced the Indians out.

Captain Gray, ordered to dislodge a large group from behind fences, charged them with his company and was mortally wounded. However, the Indians were dispersed and the troops resumed the retreat.

As soon as the British turned their backs and started their march, the Indians dashed after them, attacking from the rear, cutting down stragglers and scalping them.

Captain Dalyell, in spite of the heavy firing, ran out to attempt a rescue of a wounded sergeant. He was shot to death. There was no chance to reclaim his body.

The troops moved on at the best pace they could manage with the Indians continuing to fire at them. Major Rogers and his men had holed up in a house to cover the retreat.

Captain Grant, with his advance troops, found shelter in an orchard enclosure and waited for the center and rear troops to catch up. He sent men to occupy the houses below and finally was able to set up a line of communication with the fort.

At last all the remaining men of the detachment were assembled except Rogers and his Rangers. They were inside a house and surrounded by two hundred Indians. The armed bateaux that had gone down to the fort with the dead and wounded returned and proceeded to fire their swivel cannons toward the house where Rogers was besieged. The fire from the bateaux scattered the Indians and enabled Rogers and his men to join Grant and the rest of the detachment.

The entire group took up their retreat, falling back from house to house, with the Indians yelling and whooping from a safe distance out of gunshot range.

At eight o'clock on the morning of August 1st, 1763, after six hours of marching and fighting, the weary redcoats were admitted to the fort. They had lost fifty-nine men as against the Indians' loss of fifteen or twenty.

The body of Captain Dalyell was brought to the fort later that day by one of the French habitants.

When General Amherst received the news of Captain Dalyell's defeat and death at Bloody Run, he offered a reward of 100 pounds (approximately five hundred dollars) to the person killing Pontiac. It was a considerable sum for that time, but no one offered to collect it.

In a letter dated August 8th, 1763, Major Gladwyn reported to Sir Jeffrey Amherst:

"On the 31st, Captain Dalyell requested, as a particular favor, that I would give him the command of a party, in order to attempt the surprizal of Pontiac's camp, under cover of the night, to which I answered that I was of the opinion he (Pontiac) was too much on his guard to effect it; he (Dalyell) then said he thought I had it in my power to give him (Pontiac) a stroke, and that if I did not attempt it now, he (Pontiac) would run off, and I should never have another opportunity. This induced me to give in to the scheme contrary to my best judgment."

The victory over the British who had set out to attack his camp gave Pontiac a tremendous lift in spirit. His medicine had not lost its power — he was still the mighty chief of the Ottawas and the leader of the tribes. He sent runners through the surrounding woods to spread the news of his triumph over the redcoats. As a result of the victory at Bloody Run, warriors from the neighboring tribes began to arrive at Pontiac's camp, all ready to aid the chief in his conflict with the British.

The next few days passed with only skirmishes occurring until September 4th, when one of the most dramatic events of the siege took place.

The schooner *Huron* was returning from Niagara where she had delivered letters and dispatches. On board were her master, Horst, her mate, Jacobs, and a crew of ten, plus six Iroquois Indians who were considered friendly to the English. The Iroquois asked to be set ashore when the vessel entered the Detroit River. This request was granted and they promptly disappeared in the woods.

It is supposed they reported to Pontiac that the schooner was undermanned but it is far more likely that the chief's warriors were on the lookout for the vessel and brought the news to him.

The schooner stood up in the river until dark and then anchored nine miles below the fort to wait for a favorable wind. The men on board were on the alert but it was a dark night and at a distance of a few rods they could distinguish nothing.

With muffled oars three hundred and fifty Indians rode the current downstream and were almost upon the schooner before they were seen.

The crew got off a single cannon shot among them and then the Indians were beneath the bows and clambering up the sides of the vessel, holding their knives clenched between their teeth.

The crew fired a round with their muskets and then threw down their guns, seized spears and hatchets and met the invaders man to man. Several Indians were killed and others wounded, but this failed to stop their assault.

The vessel's master, Horst, was killed, several of the crew were disabled and the Indians were leaping over the bulwarks when the mate, Jacobs, called out to the crew to blow up the vessel.

Some of the Wyandots who were already on the deck heard the order and understood its meaning. They yelled to their companions and these gave the alarm to the whole boarding party.

In an instant the Indians, almost to a man, leaped into the water and swam in all directions to escape the threatened explosion.

Next morning, the schooner, her deck still slippery with blood and her crew showing signs of their desperate struggle in the dark, reached the fort in safety.

Later General Amherst ordered medals struck commemorating the event and presented one to each member of the crew.

15

PONTIAC LIFTS
HIS SIEGE

THE SIEGE DRAGGED ON. The British ensign still floated over Fort Detroit, and each evening the sunset gun was fired to let the vessels at the mouth of the river know the fort was still in British hands. Snipers on both sides accounted for a few casualties but there was little action. Pontiac's allies became restless.

The chief began to have misgivings. He felt that the Master-of-Life had turned his face from his red children.

The young men watched the sky for signs of approaching winter. It was almost time to go to the hunting grounds and the warriors began slipping away a few at a time. The war could wait, but furs must be gathered and meat stored for the winter.

At this time some of Pontiac's allies, even some of his own Ottawas, declared that Pontiac had lost his power and that he was no longer their great leader.

The chief, well aware of this, spent solitary hours trying to bring back his old magic. He prayed to the Master-of-Life for victory over the English.

The frigid breath of approaching winter could be felt in the air; more warriors left for the hunting grounds and the siege slowed almost to a standstill.

At the end of October, Pontiac underwent the final assault upon his crumbling empire.

A French messenger, Dequindre, came up river from the Illinois country with letters for the Ottawa chief, for Major Gladwyn and for all the French in the area.

The letters were from Major Neyon de Villiers, commander of Fort Chartres.

"Let me hear the words of my French father in the Illinois country," Pontiac asked. He listened in grim-faced silence as the message, addressed to "French Children, the Nations of the Great Lakes" was interpreted.

"The Master-of-Life has decreed peace between Great King Louis XV of France and His Majesty, British King George III. Let all the red children lay aside the war hatchet and the scalping knife and live as brothers with the British. They and the French are now one. When the warriors strike at the British, they also spill the blood of the French. Let there be peace in the Great Lakes!"

The letter also said the French would continue to share with the Indians, but from the other side of the Mississippi.

So Pontiac, the one-time King of the Great Lakes, came to the final end of his reign. He could not fight two nations of white men.

Still majestic but tight-lipped and stern, the Ottawa chief faced at last the cruel facts he had avoided for so long. The king of France had abandoned his red children. He would never lead his great army up the St. Lawrence River with flags fluttering and arms glinting in the sun. Pontiac's dream had ended.

De Villiers' letter to the French habitants confirmed his knowledge of the signing of the Peace of Paris Treaty. It also informed them that Fort de Chartres would be given up to the British as soon as they arrived.

Still stunned by this blow, Pontiac suffered an attack on his grand scheme by the forces of nature.

At the end of October a four-inch snow fell, turning the last of the warriors into hunters who took off for the hunting grounds without further ado.

On October 31, 1763, Pontiac bowed to cruel fate and asked Major Gladwyn for peace terms.

He signed a note to the major, saying, "My brother, the word which my father has sent to make peace I have accepted; all my young men have buried the hatchet. I think you will forget the bad things which have taken place for some time past. Likewise, I shall forget what you may have done to me, in order to think of nothing but good. I, the Chippewa, the Huron, we are all ready to go speak with you when you ask us. Give us an answer. I am sending this resolution to you in order that you may see it. If you are kind as I, you will make me a reply. I wish you a good day. — Pontiac."

Gladwyn granted a temporary peace until a formal treaty could be prepared and signed.

The siege ended after six months with the English in full control of Fort Detroit. The Indians went to their hunting convinced (at least for a time) that they could not stand against the white men.

Pontiac, the mighty chief of the Ottawas, who once led sixteen nations in a battle to save their lands from the invading white men, was left alone at his council fire.

Defeat was bitter to Pontiac's proud spirit, and he found it hard to swallow. He gathered the Ottawas who were still loyal to him and camped on the Maumee River. He hunted to care for his family's needs, as other braves did, and he wore the same simple clothing as the others with only one eagle feather in his hair.

But Pontiac kept the war alive in his heart and continued to plan for another try at the fort when the winter ended.

During the next few months he visited the nations far and near and made every effort to regain his power and influence. He even threatened to kill the Ottawas who wanted peace at the fort, but he realized that he had lost his grip on the other chiefs and warriors. Former comrades-in-arms were reluctant to unite with a loser.

Also, with the change in power from French to British there was much confusion all along the Mississippi River where he had hoped to recruit followers for a new war against the English.

In the spring of 1764, Pontiac's war spirit revived. He sent messengers carrying war belts to the Illinois country, along the Wabash River, and down the Mississippi to visit the tribes and gain support for renewing the war against the English. He asked the tribes to the south to stop English troops trying to move up river and invade the Illinois country.

The chief went in person to visit Neyon de Villiers, commanding officer at Fort Chartres, and ask for help.

De Villiers greeted him with a question: was the chief out of his mind? Had he not received the letter sent to Detroit last autumn? Later the commander said he could offer no help because their French father had given up the country. He confessed that he himself had asked to be recalled to France.

Then he looked into Pontiac's accusing face and asked why the chief continued to fight the British when there was no hope of success.

Pontiac replied hotly, "My warriors at Detroit will die with tomahawk in hand before they will bow to the English!"

He asked de Villiers to summon the French habitants to a meeting so he could speak to them of what was in his heart.

Pontiac made a long speech and finished it by declaring: "We will not end our war with the English as long as one of us remains alive. We ask you to beg our father, the French King, not to abandon his red children."

Neyon tried to explain that their father wished the French and the Indians to have peace with the British, but Pontiac would have none of this.

He shouted, "We hate them and we will fight them to the end."

The commander replied that it would be better if Pontiac returned to his own village rather than prolong a war that could only bring ruin and sorrow to his people. He asked the chief to come back when he had thought more about it.

16

PONTIAC MAKES PEACE WITH THE ENGLISH

PONTIAC LEFT FORT DE CHARTRES without seeing de Villiers again. He went to village after village seeking for help. He needed powder and lead as well as recruits, but most of the other tribes were also short of ammunition and were unwilling or unable to help him.

At this time the entire frontier to the east was ablaze with violence and savagery. Roving bands of Indians attacked the settlements, tomahawked the inhabitants and burned their homes. Settlers moved their families into the fortified towns and took up arms to protect their lives and property. Border ruffians, often disguised as Indians, waylaid traders and even military expeditions to rob them of their stocks.

The peace that prevailed in the Illinois country was an uneasy one with incidents occurring on the borders and in isolated places.

General Thomas Gage, who had succeeded General Amherst as commander-in-chief of the British forces in America, sent expeditions, detachments of troops and exploring parties into the Indian lands to reconcile the natives and pave the way for the British take-over. Agents of the Crown and English traders risked their lives to persuade the hostile tribesmen to make peace with the new owners of the land.

With Pontiac stirring up the Indians who lived along the Mississippi, General Gage believed that he could not reach the Illinois country by moving up the river from New Orleans. He felt the necessity of planting the English flag over the forts that still displayed the fleur-de-lis. He said that only then would the country be at peace.

General Gage's plan was to send troops from the east by way of Fort Pitt and the Ohio River. He ordered George Croghan to proceed ahead of the troops with a plentiful supply of gifts and try to win the goodwill of the Indians.

Pontiac, accompanied by his four hundred loyal young warriors, swept through the forests and along the river front. He spoke in councils, raging, warning and even threatening the tribes.

He sent messengers bearing the great wampum belt with forty-seven symbols of the bands and tribes still loyal to him down the length of the Mississippi and directed that it be shown in every camp along the way. He told them to show it then to Monsieur D'Abbadie, the governor at New Orleans and demand help for his campaign against the English. However, they found the French leaving the city ahead of the take-over. A new governor succeeded D'Abbadie, who died suddenly, and there was no prospect of any aid from that quarter.

As the French abandoned the city of New Orleans ahead of the British occupation, they sent boat-loads of goods to Kaskaskia. The shops opened for trade and the Indians flocked to them to barter and bargain. This caused the French to start up the war talk and try to sell their stock of guns and ammunition.

Each new arrival in the Illinois country seemed to circulate another rumor. The French traders, on hearing that an

English detachment was descending the Ohio River, ceased supplying the tribes with arms and ammunition. When the Indians asked about the French king's army that was coming to aid them, the traders claimed to have no knowledge of any such story.

The French commander, St. Ange, still in charge of the Illinois country, refused to give the Indians presents. He told them to look to the English for supplies and advised them to remain at peace with the new rulers.

Pontiac learned of a boat-load of goods that the English officers in the south were sending up the Mississippi River. The supplies were to be distributed among the Indians and pave the way to more friendly relations with the owners of the land.

The chief and his warriors met the boat at the river bank, lifted the cargo and divided the goods among the needy of their own.

In spite of this and other small successes, the chief now realized that even the most devoted of his followers were losing heart and falling away from him. Finally the report of his ambassadors as they returned from New Orleans without any promise of aid convinced him that his cause was a hopeless one. He could hold out no longer. He must make peace with the English — or go elsewhere.

Where?

Southward to the Cherokees — hereditary enemies of his people?

West to the Osages and the Missouri — uncertain friends, or to the fierce and jealous Dakotas?

In the east he knew the forests would soon be filled with English traders, settlers and troops, while to the north, his own village at Detroit lay under the guns of the English fort.

If he took refuge in the trackless wilderness of the upper lakes, he would have to go alone, leaving his people without a leader.

He faced the rising sun after a night of prayer and left the decision to the Master-of-Life.

When Pontiac returned to his village on the Maumee that fall, he found that some chiefs of other tribes had gone to Detroit to ask for peace. Many of his former allies were urging Pontiac's own Ottawas to move back to their old camp at Detroit.

Chief Atawang, who was the leader of the pro-British band of Ottawas, boldly declared that Pontiac no longer spoke for the Ottawas — only for his own village.

The Hurons of Detroit, along with delegations from the other tribes in the Lake Superior area were attending Sir William Johnson's conference at Fort Niagara. They said, "We do not want Pontiac or his war. Send us traders!"

Pontiac had a meeting with Minavavana, the head chief of the Chippewas, in the Illinois country. There, some of the die-hard French told the chiefs that if they would keep the British from taking over the Illinois country in the summer (1765), the French king would send (not lead) an army to aid them in the spring of 1766.

They asked if their red brothers did not know that when the British moved into the Illinois country, they would pit the Indians of the south against the northern tribes?

This was a threat that Pontiac had considered but refused to discuss. He was bitterly opposed to any British take-over and he especially did not want the British in the Illinois country. He thought that if the Ottawas were forced from their homes on the Great Lakes, they could move to the Illinois.

Pontiac went to St. Louis, newly founded by French Pierre Laclede and young Pierre Chouteau. The men told him they had abandoned their homes in New Orleans as soon as they received the news that the king of France had signed a peace treaty with Great Britain.

The chief then sought out his comrade of the French and

Indian War, St. Ange de Bellerive, who now commanded Fort Chartres on the east bank of the Mississippi.

Pontiac reminded St. Ange of the times when they fought together against the Iroquois and the English. He asked for weapons and ammunition and soldiers to help him keep out the British.

The answer he received was a disappointing one.

"The old days are gone," St. Ange replied. "You must live with the English as we have to do." He explained about the notice he had received that all the land east of the Mississippi had been signed to the British, who would soon arrive to take over his fort.

Pontiac replied heatedly, "But it is the Indians' land. We do not want the English, who build settlements everywhere. They ruin our forests and hunting grounds and my people are losing their freedom." He turned to pleading. "Cannot our French father help us?"

St. Ange put out a hand in quick sympathy for his old friend. Then he shook his head and told Pontiac that he could not assist him. "The French are finished in America," he said sadly. "The country now belongs to the British."

Pontiac knew his warriors and their families had suffered in order to follow him — now he wanted to make the best possible peace with the English, smoke the calumet with them, and go back to his camp on the Maumee River, leaving vengeance to the future.

He and his chiefs met Croghan at Ouatanon. He gave his hand to the English agent and set up a council at which the chief offered a peace belt and the calumet and joined with the Ouatanon chiefs in expressing friendship for the English.

The Ottawa chief said that the French had deceived him, telling him that the English meant to enslave the Illinois tribes and turn the Cherokees loose upon them. It was this that caused him to take up arms but now that he knew the story to be false, he would no longer stand in the path of the English.

Pontiac added stoutly that the English must not imagine that, in taking possession of the French forts, they gained any right to the country, for the French had never bought the land and lived upon it by sufferance only.

At the close of the conference, Croghan's party, followed by Pontiac and his warriors and many of the chiefs of the Illinois, set out for Fort Detroit.

The combined parties reached Detroit on August 17, 1765. They found a great gathering of Indians — Ottawas, Potawatomies and Chippewas — encamped about the fort.

The bad luck that had dogged them and the miseries they had endured from the suspension of the fur trade had taken the hostility from the minds and hearts of the warriors. They were anxious to regain favor with the English and hungry for presents and rum.

The warriors crowded into Croghan's meetings and expressed regret over their bad conduct. They said they were glad that the dark clouds (of war) were now dispersing and the sunshine of peace returning; and since all the nations to the sunrising (east) had taken their great father, the King of England, (George III) by the hand, they also wished to do the same.

They explained that they now saw that the French were indeed conquered, and that henceforth they would listen no more to the whistling of evil birds but would lay down the war hatchet and sit quiet on their mats.

The Grand Sauteur (chief of the Chippewas) said the red people had been deceived by white men and hoped the English would take pity on the women and children and grant peace to the nation.

A Potawatomie band from St. Joseph, through their orator, asked that they be excused for their past conduct and blamed it on the young men who could not be controlled.

He wound up by saying:

"Fathers, when we formerly came to visit our fathers, the French, they always sent us home joyful and we hope you, fathers, will have pity on our women and young men, who are in great want of necessities, and not let us go home to our towns ashamed (empty handed)."

On August 27th, Croghan held a meeting with Pontiac's Ottawas and the other tribes of Detroit and Sandusky.

His speech was a masterpiece of figurative language, outdoing even the Indian orators' imagery:

"Children, we are very glad to see so many of you here present at your ancient council fire (Detroit) which has been neglected for some time; since then high winds have blown and raised heavy clouds over your country. I now, by this wampum belt rekindle your ancient fire, and throw dry wood upon it, that the blaze may ascend to heaven, so that all nations may see it, and know that you live in peace and tranquility with your fathers, the English."

Croghan went on to give a wampum belt to disperse the black clouds over the heads of the Indians — another belt to gather up the bones of deceased friends — and one to take the hatchet from the hands of the warriors in order to plant a tree of peace under which the English and the Indians and their children might sit and smoke in peace.

While his listeners sat as if hypnotized, Croghan finished his oration by declaring:

"Children, we have made a road from the sunrising to the sunsetting. I desire that you will preserve the road good and pleasant to travel upon, that we may all share the blessings of his happy union."

This concluded the meeting and the Indians withdrew to discuss the points Croghan had covered and to plan their reply.

The next day Pontiac spoke in behalf of the several nations assembled at the council:

"Father, we have all smoked out of this pipe of peace. It is your children's pipe; and as the war is all over, and the Great Spirit and Giver of Light, who has made the earth and everything therein, has brought us together this day for our mutual good, I declare to all nations that I have settled my peace with you before I came here, and now deliver my pipe to be sent to Sir William Johnson, that he may know I have made peace, and taken the king of England for my father, in presence of all the nations now assembled; and whenever any of those nations go to visit him, they may smoke out of it with him in peace. Fathers, we are obliged to you for lighting up our council fire for us, and desiring us to return to it (Detroit), but we are now settled on the Miami River, not far from hence. Whenever you want us, you will find us there."

Pontiac added that the Indians loved rum and if they lodged near the fort, the warriors would get drunk and there would be quarrels. However, this wise conclusion did not keep him from ending his speech with a request that Croghan unstop the rum barrel so the thirsty warriors could have a drink.

At the end of September, Croghan wound up the long conference. Before leaving Detroit to report the success of his mission to the commander-in-chief, Croghan obtained a promise from Pontiac that the chief would go to Oswego in the spring, as soon as the ice was off the lakes, and sign a peace treaty with Sir William Johnson — as befitted one of Pontiac's importance.

In the Illinois country, a detachment of one hundred highlanders of the 42nd Regiment under Captain Sterling, descended the Ohio River from Fort Pitt to Fort Chartres, lowered the French flag which flew over the fort, and raised the British emblem. French commander St. Ange gave up his post and the English occupied the land.

17

PONTIAC GOES TO THE HAPPY HUNTING GROUNDS

FOR PONTIAC, the winter of 1765-1766 passed quietly. The partial reopening of the fur trade brought relief to the tribes from the famine and want of the previous year. The hunters were allowed ammunition and no longer were forced to rely on the half-forgotten skills of their forefathers with bows and arrows and lances.

When spring came, Pontiac kept the promise he had made to Croghan to visit Sir William Johnson at Oswego and sign the peace treaty.

The chief left his camp on the Maumee accompanied by his entourage of chiefs wearing their finest ceremonial outfits. When the sixty gaily decorated birch canoes reached Oswego (New York), they were saluted by the booming of cannon and Sir William Johnson greeted them with outstretched hand. Johnson had with him the chief sachems of the Iroquois whom he had invited to attend in order to give prestige and color to the occasion.

Johnson concluded his lengthy speech by offering a wampum belt and saying:

"Children, I now, by this belt, turn your eyes to the sunrising (east), where you will always find me your sincere friend. From me you will always hear what is good and true; and I charge you never more to listen to those evil birds, who come with lying tongues, to lead you astray, and to make you break the solemn engagements which you have entered into, in the presence of the Great Spirit, with the king, your father, and the English people. Be strong, then, and keep fast hold of the chain of friendship, that your children, following your example, may live happy and prosperous lives."

Pontiac, in a brief reply, promised to answer in full in the next session and the meeting broke up.

The council of the next day was opened by the Wyandot chief, Teata, who made a short formal address.

Then Pontiac rose and addressed Johnson as follows:

"Father, when our great father of France was in this country, I held him fast by the hand. Now that he is gone, I take you, my English father, by the hand, in the name of all the nations, and promise to keep this covenant as long as I shall live."

The chief then delivered an elaborate belt of wampum and continued:

"Father, when you address me, it is the same as if you addressed all the nations of the west. Father, this belt is to cover and strengthen our chain of friendship and to show you that, if any nation shall lift the hatchet against our English brethren, we shall be the first to feel it and resent it."

Pontiac then expressed full agreement with Sir William Johnson's wishes.

In succeeding days of the conference, details relating to the fur trade were settled to the satisfaction of all the Indians present.

Pontiac promised to recall the war belts he had sent to the north and west. He added that, when all were gathered up, they would be more than a man could carry.

Following this, the Iroquois sachems addressed Pontiac and his chiefs, advising them to stand true to their engagements and hold fast the chain of friendship with the English.

The council closed on July 31st, with Sir William Johnson distributing a bountiful supply of presents to Pontiac and his followers.

Pontiac, his canoe loaded with gifts from his once sworn enemies, the English, went home to his camp on the Maumee.

To the chief, it meant the final end of his reign as *King of the Great Lakes.* He had publicly bowed to the English conquerors and renounced forever the great plan by which he had hoped to save for his people their tribal lands and their way of life.

Nothing was left to him except to watch while the tribes scattered and the English possessed the land.

In the spring of 1769, Pontiac had an urge to see his old friends. The tribes had always met at this time of year to dance, feast and tell tales and to visit at the forts. He decided to go to see St. Ange, then commanding at St. Louis, who was one of his oldest friends among the white men.

Pontiac wanted to appear at his best when he saw St. Ange, so he dressed carefully in the white and gold uniform of a French officer which General Montcalm had given him years before.

Like many another fighting man, he found that the uniform had grown tighter over the years, but he put it on and wore it into the fort.

St. Ange, now gray-haired, greeted the chief with a hearty handshake and then asked why he had taken the risk of wearing a French uniform. "Don't you know the English still view you with concern? They might accuse you of starting the war all over again!"

Pontiac replied that he wore the white and gold to honor

his old friend, St. Ange. He said he did not fear the English, for he had taken them by the hand and said he would do them no harm.

At the feast which St. Ange held for Pontiac, the commander invited his officers and the chiefs of the nearby tribes. It was a great occasion for Pontiac, the former leader, and his heart was lighter than it had been for many moons.

After a few days of being entertained by St. Ange and young Pierre Chouteau, a leader of the townspeople, Pontiac learned that there was to be an Indian meeting at the village of Cahokia, across the Mississippi from St. Louis. He was invited to attend and take part in the *Dance-of-Chiefs*, and consented to do so.

St. Ange tried to keep the chief from going to Cahokia where the English were firmly established, but Pontiac was eager to see his old friends and insisted on going to the meeting.

The chief and his friends, unarmed, crossed the river in canoes with their families, and landed at the village of Cahokia.

The visitors were greeted by a rabble of Indians and the few white traders who lived with them in the dilapidated houses of the ruined fort. Pontiac's heart sank as he saw to what depth the once strong and self-reliant Indians had fallen. He wished he had not come to Cahokia.

That night Pontiac and his people were the honored guests at a feast held by the three tribes of the Illinois — the Kaskaskias, the Cahokias and the Peorias.

When his turn to speak came, he shamed the Illinois tribes for their idleness and the disorder he saw about him. He told them they did not have to follow the white man's ways. They could live as their forefathers had lived and find all their needs in the forests and rivers as the Master-of-Life had intended them to do. Then they would be strong and proud.

Instead of the cheers he expected, this speech brought

only head-shaking and laughter from the rag-tag crowd. It was evident they did not take his words seriously.

There was firewater passed around among the braves at the feast. Pontiac drowned his doubts and fears and kept silent.

He left the firelight and walked toward the woods singing his lucky war-chant — alone, yet not alone. Behind him walked a Peoria Indian who had been bribed to do away with the chief before he could spread his gospel of hard work and primitive living.

The Peoria raised his club and struck. Pontiac fell to the ground. The Peoria struck again with his tomahawk. And with that the chief of the Ottawas joined his slain warriors in death.

Two of Pontiac's men had trailed him when he left the council fire. They found his lifeless body where it had fallen beneath the blows of the Peoria. The assassin sought refuge among his people, and the Illinois refused to deliver him for punishment. Unarmed as they were, Pontiac's friends could only take to their canoes and return to St. Louis, where they reported the outrage to St. Ange. The commander sent soldiers to Cahokia to recover the body of his old friend and made arrangements for the chief's burial near the fort.

Pontiac was interred in the splendid white and gold uniform he treasured. He was accorded full military honors amid the wailing of the squaws and the mourning of his many friends and relatives.

Then the news was spread swiftly to warriors of the Ottawa, Ojibway and Potawatomie tribes, to the Sac and Fox and the Wyandot and to the other nations which Pontiac had led. Many came in answer to the call and pledged to avenge the Chief's death by hunting down the Illinois and wiping them from the earth. It is reported that for years the tribes of the Illinois were harassed by Pontiac's men, some of whom had never seen the chief. The glory of his name was reason enough for them to join in punishing his murderers.

The Death of Pontiac

So Pontiac, the great chief of the Ottawas, passed with his
era. His heroic spirit still hovers over the Great Lakes, trailing
a wampum belt made long and broad to contain the telling of
his brave deeds, his glorious victories and his courageous fight
to keep the homeland of his people.

ADDENDA

Pᴏɴᴛɪᴀᴄ's ᴡᴀʀ and his siege of Detroit were of such prime significance in the early history of our country that a closer look at the scene, the events and the men who opposed each other is offered herein.

When the French surrendered Montreal to General Amherst on September 8, 1760, all of Canada along with the other French possessions in the New World passed to the British.

It was a rich prize for the new ruler of Great Britain, King George III, who ascended the throne on October 26, 1760.

The end of the war caused great confusion throughout the Great Lakes area. There was bitter antagonism between the French and the conquering English. There were long delays before official orders could be carried out and the French garrisons in the surrendered forts replaced by English troops.

This period also marked the beginning of the struggle of the Indians against the whites, particularly the British. The Indians saw their lands transferred from one foreign monarch to another without regard to their native rights. They saw the country overrun by settlers.

Politically wise, Pontiac realized that the tribes would be pushed farther and farther from their homes on the lakes and their entire way of life destroyed.

Pontiac's siege of Fort Detroit was his answer to the Indians' question, "How can we dislodge the English and reclaim our land?" When fate denied him the victory and he was forced to lift his siege at the end of October, 1763, the last organized resistance to the British faded.

After the French had given up their possessions, the Mississippi River was set as the western boundary of British domain. The Ohio Valley and the nearby area was left to the Indians. By a later proclamation the whites were prohibited from moving into it. The proclamation proved to be merely a scrap of paper against a flood of land-hungry settlers. When Pontiac lifted his siege of Detroit, the forts that had been overrun during Pontiac's War were restored and garrisoned with English troops. New forts were built to control the Indians' resistance to the change-over.

In the meantime, English settlers moved into the land, English fur traders took over the French fur routes, and English became the official language of the country.

Pontiac has been described as a stalwart and commanding figure. Certainly he was big, strong and determined, and possessed the competitive spirit of a true leader. In addition he was a great warrior, an orator unmatched among his people, and a strategist of courage and resources. Even his enemies respected and envied his talent for planning and organizing resistance to white domination.

There were others of Pontiac's warriors who had fine physique and great courage, but none of them had his gift of oratory. None of them had the ability to plan and carry on a campaign such as the six-month siege of Fort Detroit.

In the turbulent year of 1760 and for the next decade, the time and the Indians' cause demanded a seasoned fighter and a farseeing leader. Pontiac nominated himself for the job. He was in his prime, around forty-four years old, when he set up the *Confederation of Indian Nations* that led to the siege of Fort Detroit. This siege, the longest continuous one in Indian history, held the English pinned down in the fort from the first of May, 1763, to the end of October, during which time the British garrison kept a weary day and night watch, often on short rations.

The significance of the result of this drawn-out battle between Pontiac and English Major Gladwyn, commander of the fort, can hardly be overestimated. The future of our northeast territory and possibly our entire country was at stake. If Pontiac had been able to take over Fort Detroit, our country might now be a French colony and our language French. Voila!

AMHERST

Pontiac's most implacable enemy, though they had little actual contact with each other, was Sir Jeffrey Amherst, Commander-in-Chief of the British forces in America.

General Amherst feared and hated Pontiac. Seeing the Ottawa chief as the main point of resistance to British control, he called him "an ignorant savage," and made every effort to destroy his power and influence among the Indians.

Sir Jeffrey Amherst was born at Sevenoaks, Kent, England, January 29, 1717. He began his illustrious military career as a page boy to Lord Ligonier. He died a field marshal at the age of 80 in his birthplace of Sevenoaks. In 1758, Amherst was chosen by William Pitt (British Secretary of State) and Lord Ligonier (then Duke of Cumberland) to command in Canada.

On July 26, 1758, forces under Amherst's command captured Louisburg on Breton Island, Nova Scotia.

After this important victory, Amherst was promoted to commander-in-chief in America.

It was General Amherst who planned the three-pronged attack on Quebec that resulted in the capture of that French stronghold in 1759.

Montreal, on the St. Lawrence River, was surrendered to Amherst's British forces on September 8, 1760, allowing Canada and all French possessions in America to pass into the hands of the British Crown.

Amherst remained in Canada as governor general until late in 1763.

General Amherst was considered a courageous officer and a brilliant commander. His victories over the French were lauded throughout the British empire.

However, his relations with the natives, and particularly Pontiac, proved that he had little understanding of the Indians and less sympathy for their plight. They were nuisances to him and he begrudged every cent spent for their welfare.

When General Amherst's request for transfer to England was complied with, he left his Indian troubles on his desk for his successor, General Gage, to worry over and sailed for London, hoping never to see another Indian.

He acted as commander-in-chief of the British army from 1772 to 1775. During the war with the American colonists his tactics were unsuccessful.

He became a baron in 1776, and a field marshal in 1790. He died at Sevenoaks the next year.

Amherst College, established in 1821 at Amherst, Massachusetts, was so named in his honor.

CROGHAN

George Croghan's name had power throughout the Great Lakes region during the mid-1700's. Pontiac knew him well.

Irish-born Croghan was the most important English fur-trader in the area. He was also an agent of the Pennsylvania government to handle business of the state and a deputy to General Amherst, second to Sir William Johnson.

In 1750, Croghan and other English traders were trying to capture the French trade in furs. The French routes ranged from Quebec to Louisiana and yielded a yearly total of many thousands of dollars.

Charles Langlade, a French-Indian from Green Bay, led an expedition of over two hundred Ottawas and Chippewas to Pickawillany, Ohio, in 1752 and destroyed the English fur-trading market there, forcing Croghan and his associates back to Pennsylvania.

The French at that time offered a reward of one thousand dollars for Croghan's scalp. The Irish trader had cut into the French trade routes by sending out men with trains of pack horses. Each pack horse was loaded with trade goods — ammunition, cloth, blankets, kettles and knives, and most desired of all, rum.

By offering these in trade the English traders were able to meet the Indians en route to the French gathering places and skim off the cream of fine furs. Most of the natives were over-eager to get their hands on the small articles such as mirrors, whistles, beads and other trifles that appealed to their tastes, without much consideration as to their value.

George Croghan was a bold operator, a sharp trader, and, as second to Johnson in handling Indian affairs, a very busy man. He moved about among the tribes, always with plenty of trade goods to use as small gifts as well as to purchase furs for his own private business. He also carried messages and exercised considerable authority with the Indians. They trusted him, often to their sorrow.

Although he did not have the genuine liking for the natives that Johnson showed, and was committed to English control of the country, Croghan worked to establish peace between the tribes and their conquerors. He saw it as the only solution to the Indians' problems.

GLADWYN

Pontiac's direct opponent in the battle for Fort Detroit was Lieutenant Henry Gladwyn (later Major Gladwyn), commander of the fort — a handsome, fair-haired young Englishman who took part in the Braddock Battle in 1755 and was wounded in that action.

The rout of the British troops in that fight may have led Pontiac to think that the British lacked the stamina to outlast a long siege. However, the chief learned to his sorrow that Major Gladwyn was made of stern stuff. His heroic stand at Fort Detroit is a classic example of British bull-dog courage and endurance.

In the face of threats by Pontiac that the kettle for boiling the major and his garrison was already on the fire, Gladwyn refused to consider giving up his post. He sent word to Pontiac that he would hold it as long as he had a single man left to defend it.

These were brave words in view of the fact that the garrison was short of food and most of his troops wanted to take the easy way out by abandoning the fort.

Their commander's stout-fellow attitude encouraged the besieged garrison to make the best of their predicament. Gladwyn took what safety measures he could — such as having tubs of water set along the inside walls of the fort at intervals so fire arrows thrown inside the fort could be hastily put out. He sent messages asking for reinforcements and food and kept the British ensign flying over the fort to let the vessels anchored in the Detroit River know he was still holding out.

In September of 1763, Gladwyn gained his promotion to Lieutenant Colonel. When the siege was finally lifted and a measure of peace restored in the area, Gladwyn, thoroughly sick of the whole place and the situation, was forced to spend another winter at Fort Detroit before he could be relieved of the command. He then collected his back pay and sailed for England where he lived the good life of a country gentleman with not an Indian in sight.

JOHNSON

One of the most important men in the British service during Pontiac's war and later was William Johnson, an Irish fur-
trader who emigrated to New York in 1738 and settled in the
Mohawk Valley.

He built a make-shift trading post and began trading with
the Iroquois Indians, treating them fairly and maintaining
friendly relations with them. He persuaded them to side with
the English.

Johnson learned to communicate with the Iroquois in the
area, adopted some of their customs and took a Mohawk girl
for his second wife after his first wife died. The Mohawks
gave him a title — *Chief Much Busy*.

When the French and Indian war began in 1754, Johnson
was commissioned a major general and led his British and Indian (Iroquois) troops into conflict with the French. His
ability as an organizer helped to win a victory at Lake George
in 1755, thus protecting Albany (New York) from capture
and the Mohawk Valley from invasion by the French. For his
services in this action Johnson was awarded a baronetcy and as
Sir William Johnson became a wealthy landowner with three
fine homes where he often entertained his Indian friends and
held council.

Recognizing Sir William Johnson's skill as a diplomat and
organizer, Sir Jeffrey Amherst, commander-in-chief of the
British forces in the New World, appointed Johnson as his
deputy in charge of Indian affairs and sent him to handle the
delicate matter of making peace with the hostile tribes.

Amherst's idea was to quiet the natives and obtain peace as
cheaply as possible. He did not believe it necessary to give the

Indians presents to guarantee their good behavior. He said he expected them to behave themselves and if they did not, they would be punished.

Sir William Johnson had a better understanding of the natives and their problems. He asked for easier terms for them, more ammunition and clothing, and more rum for their celebrations.

Finally, in 1766, it was Sir William Johnson who negotiated terms with the tribes and signed a peace treaty with Pontiac himself.

ACKNOWLEDGMENTS

Little, Brown & Co., Boston, Mass.
   For permission to use excerpts from
   The Conspiracy of Pontiac by Francis Parkman
   Illustration: The Death of Pontiac
      Painting by De Cost Smith
Pontiac Motor Division, General Motors Corp., Pontiac, Michigan
      Courtesy: C. L. Cousins, Service Promotion Manager
      Illustrations: Indians and French Canadians
      The Wampum Maker
      The Ritual of the Calumet
      Pontiac meets with Major Robert Rogers
Burton Historical Collection, Detroit Public Library
      Courtesy: James M. Babcock, Chief
      Maps: Carte des Cinq Grands Lacs du Canada
      Plan of Fort Detroit, 1760
      Illustrations: "Conspiracy of Pontiac Revealed —"
         Painting by John Mix Stanley
         Photograph by Joseph Klima, Jr., Detroit Institute of Arts
New York Public Library, Prints Division
      Illustrations: Major Robert Rogers
      General Sir Jeffrey Amherst
         Engraving by J. Scott
      Indians Playing Lacrosse
         Painting by George Catlin
Library of Congress Photoduplication Service
      Illustrations: Major George Croghan
      Sir William Johnson
         Engraving by Charles Spooner after portrait by T. Adams
      Major Henry Gladwyn
         Painting by John Holland

BIBLIOGRAPHY

Bunce, W. H.	War Belts of Pontiac	
New York, N.Y.	E. P. Dutton & Co.	1942
Hays, Wilma P.	Pontiac, Lion in the Forest	
Boston, Mass.	Houghton Mifflin Co.	1965
Jones, Evan	Trappers and Mountain Men	
New York, N.Y.	American Heritage Pub. Co.	1961
Josephy, Alvin M.	The Patriot Chiefs	
New York, N.Y.	Viking Press	1961
La Farge, Oliver	The American Indian	
New York, N.Y.	Golden Press	1960
Leavitt, Dr. Jerome S.	America and Its Indians	
New York, N.Y.	Grossett & Dunlap	1962
McSpadden, J. W.	Indian Heroes	
New York, N.Y.	Thomas Y. Crowell Co.	1928
Parkman, Francis	The Conspiracy of Pontiac	
Boston, Mass.	Little, Brown and Co.	1870-1902
Peckham, Howard H.	Pontiac and the Indian Uprising	
Princeton, N.J.	University Press	1947
Quaife, Milo Milton	The Siege of Detroit in 1763	
Chicago, Ill.	R. R. Donnelly Sons & Co.	1958
Sabin, Edwin L.	Boys' Book of Indian Warriors	
Philadelphia, Pa.	Geo. W. Jacobs & Co.	1918
Van Every, Dale	Forth to the Wilderness	
New York, N.Y.	William Morrow & Co.	1962
Wellman, Paul I.	Indian Wars and Warriors East	
Boston, Mass.	Houghton Mifflin Co.	1959

INDEX

147

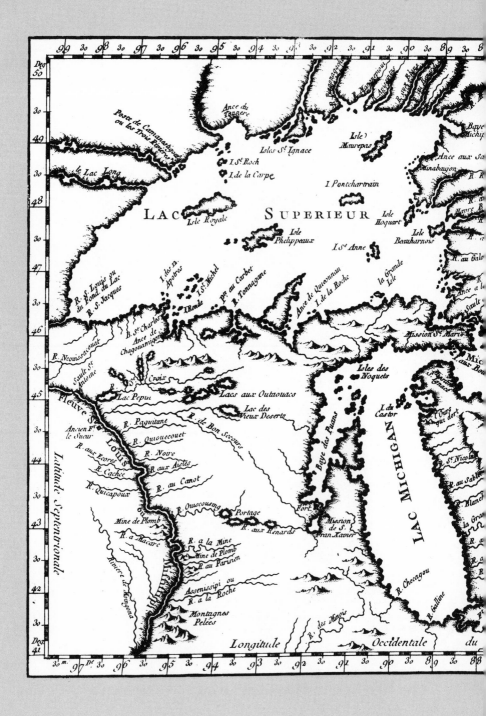